Outdoor Play for 1-

We are all mindful of the increasing news coverage of outdoor play and its benefits, but how can you go beyond the sandpit and hopscotch to create a magical and creative experience for the children in your care?

This book provides all the encouragement you will need to set up and run an outdoor toddler group. It provides a step-by-step guide to selecting an appropriate site, resourcing the outside area, devising age-appropriate activities, planning activities and the legal requirements involved. Including an overview of the developmental milestones of babies and toddlers, it shows you how you can meet their specific needs.

Features include:

- an activity bank full of games, suggestions for crafts, Forest School activities and songs and stories;
- practical advice on risk assessment and health and safety;
- guidance on working with parents and carers;
- adaptable planning templates.

With a strong emphasis on providing fun learning activities throughout the year, this book will be essential reading for all those that want to provide high quality outdoor experiences for the youngest children in their care.

Isabel Hopwood-Stephens is a qualified teacher and OCN Level 3 Forest School Leader. She has run many groups and school trips specialising in Forest School activities for children, from pre-school outdoor parent and toddler groups to eleven year olds in after-school clubs.

Outdoor Play for 1–3 Year Olds

How to set up and run your own outdoor toddler group

Isabel Hopwood-Stephens

Routledge
Taylor & Francis Group

LONDON AND NEW YORK

First published 2015
by Routledge
2 Park Square, Milton Park, Abingdon, Oxon OX14 4RN

and by Routledge
711 Third Avenue, New York, NY 10017

Routledge is an imprint of the Taylor & Francis Group, an informa business

British Library Cataloguing in Publication Data
A catalogue record for this book is available from the British Library

Library of Congress Cataloging in Publication Data
Hopwood-Stephens, Isabel.
   Outdoor play for 1–3 year olds: how to set up and run your own outdoor
   toddler group/Isabel Hopwood-Stephens.
   1. Play groups. 2. Outdoor games. 3. Play environments.
   4. Infants—Development. 5. Toddlers—Development.
   I. Title. II. Title: Outdoor play for one to three year olds.
   LB1140.35.P55H67 2014
   372.21—dc23
   2014013907

ISBN: [978–1–138–77851–1] (hbk)
ISBN: [978–1–138–77852–8] (pbk)
ISBN: [978–1–315–77194–6] (ebk)

Typeset in Optima
by Swales and Willis Ltd, Exeter, Devon

Printed and bound in Great Britain by
TJ International Ltd, Padstow, Cornwall

Contents

1   Outdoor learning: what it is and why it matters   1

Welcome to this book   1
What is outdoor learning and why is it important?   1
What is an outdoor toddler group like?   5
What will I find out from reading the rest of this book?   6

2   Working with 1–3 year olds   8

Developmental milestones   8
How young children learn   10
The role of play in learning   13
How this relates to your activity planning   14
Typical behaviours and what they might mean   14

3   Getting your site ready   18

What kind of thing am I looking for?   18
Things to consider   19
Possible sites   20
Existing childcare settings   21
Preparing for a meeting with the site representative   21
Preparing the site   24

4   What will I need?   29

Finding resources   29
Resource collections   30
Record-keeping   33
Insurance   35

Contents

First aid   35
What qualifications will I need?   35
Tax affairs   36

5   **Staying safe and having fun**   37

Going out in all weathers   37
Other essentials   38
Dealing with extremes   40
Providing shelter   42
Adult-to-child ratios   43
Site boundaries   43
Risk assessment   44
Accidents and emergencies   45

6   **Spread the word!**   48

Offline publicity   48
Online   49
By phone   51
Communication with parents   51
Working with parents: a positive relationship   53

7   **Planning**   55

Different group types   55
How to plan   56

8   **Activity bank**   60

Games and physical activities   61
Craft and creative activities   79
Songs   117
Planning activities for one year olds (infants)   117
Using storybooks   122
Thematic planning   122

9   **Useful links**   124

Sources of funding   125
Equipment providers   125
Finding a site   125
Guidance on tax, self-employment and paying others   127
Disclosure and Barring Service (formerly CRB checks)   127

First aid training   127
Safeguarding children   128
Early Years Foundation Stage statutory framework   128
Insurers specialising in childcare settings   128
Developing your grounds   128
Further activity ideas   129
Forest School training and forestry information   130

Planning Template 1   131
Planning Template 2   132
Planning Template 3   133
Appendix: Risk assessment grid   134
Bibliography   137

1 Outdoor learning
What it is and why it matters

Welcome to this book

I hope that this book provides all the encouragement you will need to set up your own outdoor toddler group, whether as an interested parent or a childcare professional. From selecting an appropriate site and devising age-appropriate activities, to tips on staffing, working with parents and legal requirements involved, it offers a range of useful advice. It also gives an overview of the developmental milestones of children aged between one and three years, and offers guidance on how to meet their specific needs. I hope that you find it a useful and stimulating resource that sets you off on your own adventure!

In this chapter we will look at:

- what outdoor learning is and why it's important;
- the benefits of playing and learning outside;
- some developmental benefits to children in the 1–3 years age range;
- some common myths and misunderstandings about outdoor learning;
- an outline of the different types of outdoor-group formats;
- a quick guide to what you'll find in the rest of this book.

What is outdoor learning and why is it important?

To answer this question we need to look at our evolving understanding of outdoor learning and the ethos of the Forest School movement, before examining how it benefits young children in the 1–3 years age range.

History of Forest School

It has long been recognised that activity is beneficial for children of all ages, hence the regular timetabling of PE for school children and an emphasis on participating in sport during free time. Pre-school children are also included in this: local playgrounds are thronged with parents and children at the weekends, and there has been a rise in the number of indoor "soft play" venues for children under the age of five to bounce around.

But until relatively recently, there was little acknowledgement of the value of creative, imaginative play in a natural outdoor setting. This was perhaps because, for previous generations, access to wild areas and the freedom to roam was just as much a part of childhood as school and the tooth fairy.

In the last decade, however, children have had their freedom to roam and explore curtailed in many ways, and for many good reasons: concerns about child abduction, traffic and the growing scarcity of undeveloped woodland or wasteland sites have all played a part. Educational and developmental experts have queued up to tell us how our children are suffering from a lack of contact with nature (Louv, 2008). So parents are now faced with a dilemma: how can I provide the freedoms that I experienced for my own children in today's world?

During the past two decades, the Forest School model of learning has been gaining ground in the UK. The Forest School teaching method that started in post-war Scandinavia has evolved into a worldwide educational movement, but in its original form it taught children practical outdoor skills, songs and stories alongside an appreciation of nature and community.

In its current form in the UK, the Forest School model for learning has been adopted by education authorities who value its impact on the social, emotional and cognitive development of children (Pilsbury, 2008). It has also been adopted and practised by many childcare practitioners and Early Years leaders who value its holistic approach to child development.

In essence, it fosters children's social, emotional, cognitive and behavioural development through regular opportunities to explore and interact with the natural environment. Activities are led by trained practitioners and are designed to be open-ended, creative and to provide opportunities for collaborative working and reflection (Hopwood-Stephens, 2012). Children are encouraged to explore their own ideas rather than imitating the leader by experimenting with different approaches to solving a problem, such as finding suitable materials to make the roof on a shelter. The activities in this book have their roots in the Forest School ethos and focus on simple, creative activities that young children can participate in and enjoy.

Benefits of playing and learning outside

When we think about playing and learning outside, we need to get past the "weather factor". A pioneering outdoor kindergarten in Sweden called I Ur Och Skur (Come Rain or Shine) goes out in all weathers. There is even a Swedish saying that there is no such thing as bad weather, just bad clothing! (Robertson, 2008).

Wrapped up in waterproofs and wellies, children don't really care about rain – what they notice is the colours, textures, sensations on their skin and the sounds of wildlife. As long as they are warm and mostly dry, they will happily play for ages. Restricting our children's exploration of the outdoors to when it's sunny and warm is misguided at best and neglectful at worst, because they miss out on a multi-sensory experience at a critical stage in the development of their cognitive, motor, spatial and communication skills (Keenan and Evans, 2009).

Of course, it's not just the sensory stimulation that children and babies get from being outside. It's also the experience of being in the open with space to crawl, toddle or even run. In other words, that sensation of freedom (Bilton, 2002) which most of us would find impossible to replicate within the confines of our house or backyard. They also get the opportunity to examine things closely, discover the natural world and familiarise themselves with a landscape (Bache, 2008).

So why the interest in trees and woods, rather than just going to the park or walking to the shops? Research indicates that the more trees and green space is available, the more the children will play (Taylor et al., 1998), and for longer, with games of greater complexity and imagination (Henninger, 1985), thus developing their social skills and language. There is also the option to manipulate and interact with their surroundings in a way which may not be possible in a private garden or manicured park – piling up branches and twigs to make a shelter for example, or picking flowers to decorate a nest made of grass clippings.

Evidence suggests that we all find visits to woodland restorative and stress-reducing (Forestry Commission Scotland, 2005), and research into nursery and infant-school children found that those enjoying regular outdoor activity had lower levels of stress hormone cortisol and took fewer days off through illness (Dahlgren and Szczepanski, 1998; Grahn et al., 1997).

From the child's perspective, every day dawns with the possibility of new discoveries about their world. Infants and children learn by doing. When children are investigating their ideas outside, the usual restrictions on mess, noise and space that they encounter when playing indoors are no longer a problem, giving them more freedom to pursue their ideas.

Babies and children in the 1–3-year-old range

Learning and playing in the natural environment can be incredibly beneficial to a child's development, even from a young age. A more detailed outline of child development theory and how it relates to outdoor play is given in Chapter 2, but some of the benefits to early development are summarised below:

Motor: in essence, babies develop and use simple schemes of movement when they are learning how to move their bodies. As young children, they refine and combine their schemes to learn how to execute more complex and extended movements. The opportunity to handle a wide range of objects of differing materials, sizes, weights and textures helps infants to refine and develop their skills of grasping, holding and placing objects. As they become more mobile, playing on uneven ground and the opportunity to climb on stones and logs helps to develop motor co-ordination better than playing on flat ground (Grahn et al., 1997).

Communication and language: playing and learning in a different environment, such as the woods, exposes children to a range of new vocabulary to describe what they can see, hear, feel, taste and smell. These words, often coming from a trusted adult carer, enrich a child's developing understanding of the world and are given concrete meaning through being introduced in context, e.g. *frost, prickly, magpie*.

Regular outdoor play and exploration of open space can also introduce children to location vocabulary such as *above, under, behind, over there, by, behind, in front*.

Spatial awareness: a child's sense of spatial awareness is most easily thought of as their awareness of where they are within a space in relation to the other things within it. As already discussed, playing in open spaces with varied terrain will provide plenty of opportunity to hear words and phrases used to describe the position of other people and things in relation to the child. Exploring these spaces and mentally comparing locations of different objects and people in relation to themselves will also help develop this awareness.

Social: babies and small children are only aware of their own needs initially, and are not able to put themselves in the shoes of others to imagine their thoughts or feelings. Being part of communal activities is fascinating to them nevertheless, as they are able to watch and imitate their peers' actions. For children with highly kinaesthetic learning styles, watching and imitating the actions of someone else can be a more effective way of learning than listening to instructions.

Cognitive: children who attended the outdoor nursery in the study cited by Grahn et al. (1997) showed higher levels of concentration when attending to tasks indoors as the children in the ordinary nursery. They also played more imaginatively, inventing a wider range of games which lasted for longer.

Health: as counter-intuitive as it might sound, exposure to microbes and germs is an essential part of developing a healthy immune system to fight off infection. This doesn't mean that we need to bathe our children in mud! But it does mean that playing only in well-cleaned indoor environments prevents their immune systems from developing as robustly as they might. Furthermore, spending time outside in a natural environment can be a relaxing, recharging experience for adults. There is no reason to assume that the same does not apply to children.

"But we've only got a small patch of grass . . ."

I hope that this book dispels two pernicious myths about outdoor learning for children. The first is that outdoor toddler groups are things that happen on the posh side of town, in acres of beautiful outdoor space filled with trees and expensive wooden play equipment. Not true! All you need to start with is a yard with a patch of grass, some cheap resources and some enthusiastic play leaders. Worrying that what we have available might not be "good enough" can sometimes hold us back from providing a perfectly decent outdoor facility for children to play and learn.

The second is that playing outdoors is inherently dangerous. Also not true. In the words of Lindon (1999), "a well-intentioned focus on keeping children as safe as possible has shifted towards looking for anything and everything that can go wrong."

Some of the risks are different to playing inside, but with sensible planning these can be minimised. More importantly, the benefits are enormous, and the outdoor environment provides a wealth of sensory stimulation and adventure for children that we simply cannot hope to replicate indoors. A guide to risk assessment is given in Chapter 5.

What is an outdoor toddler group like?

Types

The four types of groups which will be discussed in this book are as follows:

Childcare setting group

By this, I mean an outdoor toddler group led by professional childcare practitioners, such as childminders or nursery workers. There would be no parents in attendance and it is likely that the group would run for forty-five minutes to one hour as part of that nursery/childminder group's scheduled activity for the day. This type of session might have a theme and children would participate in a series of activities over the course of the session.

Childcare setting carousel

This type of group is similar to above, with a key difference that various activities are taking place simultaneously within the outdoor setting, each led by a different childcare practitioner. The children would be able to move around the different activities and try them out during the allotted time.

Drop-in carousel

This type of group is one where parents accompany their children, and can arrive whenever they want during an allotted time period, participating in some or all of the activities available before leaving when they wish. This type of group tends to run for an hour and a half to two hours to maximise the number of people attending. Each member of staff will have an activity which they run on repeat during the session, as parents and children wander around choosing what to do next.

Parent and toddler group

This type of group has a fixed start and end time for all children and parents attending and tends to start and end with everyone together for songs, stories and so on. The middle part of the session might have different activities running in parallel or all children following a series of activities based around a theme. Parents are expected to help their children with activities throughout the session, although there is freedom to just explore the surroundings instead.

Independently run, no parents

Parents drop their children off at the group and then collect them afterwards, but this type of group is run independently of any existing childcare setting. Be aware that this type of group is the most complicated to set up and run. All adults working with you (and there will be some, due to regulations about adult to child ratios – see Chapter 5 for more details) need to hold appropriate childcare qualifications to work with this age range, as well as having clean Disclosure and Barring Service (DBS) checks. You will also need to find out how to register them as your employees if you are paying them, follow any relevant employer legislation and hold insurance to cover all staff.

The benefits and disadvantages of each of these formats will be discussed further in Chapter 6.

What will I find out from reading the rest of this book?

You may be relieved – or disappointed – to hear that reading this book won't turn you into a latter day Ray Mears, living in the woods and knitting trousers out of nettle stalks.

What you *will* find in the remaining chapters is a practical guide to setting up your own outdoor toddler group. I intend to steer you through the process, providing information, ideas and guidance to help you decide on what will work best for your setting and your circumstances. Here's what the following chapters offer: in Chapter 2, we will consider developmental milestones for this age range, how young children learn, the role of play in learning, how this relates to planning activities for your group and how to deal with some typical behaviours for this age range. In Chapter 3 we look at what to consider when choosing a site and possible places to start, preparing for a meeting with the site owner/representative, site preparation and activity zoning. Chapter 4 focuses upon where to find resources, suggestions for resource collections and storage, requirements for first aid, insurance and qualifications, and tax affairs you may need to consider. In Chapter 5 we look at what clothing you and the children will need, and safety considerations to going out in all kinds of weathers, providing shelter, adult-to-child ratios, risk assessment, accidents, emergencies and evacuation procedures. Chapter 6 concentrates on how to market your group offline and online, communication with parents and carers, how to write Information Sheets and Joining Letters and creating a positive relationship with parents. In Chapter 7 we consider different group types and their planning requirements, looking at different planning formats and templates to suit your group. We also consider reflecting on outcomes to get the most from your planning and health and safety information you might provide. Chapter 8 includes a huge activity bank of possible activities for your group, plus guidance on planning activities for one year olds and using storybooks for thematic planning. Finally, Chapter 9 provides links for information about sources of funding, equipment providers, finding a site, guidance on tax matters, obtaining a Disclosure and Barring Service check, first aid training and safeguarding, guidance on the Early Years Foundation Stage framework, specialist insurers, developing your activity area, sources for further activity ideas and how to find out about Forest School training. The Appendices contain templates for planning and risk assessment, which you can use or adapt as you wish.

2 Working with 1–3 year olds

In this chapter we will look at:

- developmental milestones for this age range;
- how young children learn;
- the role of play in learning;
- how this relates to planning activities for your group;
- typical behaviours, what they mean and how to deal with them.

Developmental milestones

The rate of development taking place within the body and mind of growing baby is phenomenal, and the pace doesn't let up as they turn into a toddler! It is widely accepted that developmental stages are *universal*, in that they apply to children across all cultural backgrounds (Piaget, 1926). The rate at which each child moves through each stage varies quite widely, however, and can be due to many factors including genetic predisposition, home environment, attachment to the primary caregiver and cultural norms.

Suffice to say that any summary of what children can do at different ages should be read as a general guideline, and the table which follows is no different. It outlines some of the developmental milestones that most children will have reached by the ages of one, two or three years in various spheres of development.

Table 2.1 Developmental milestones for children aged 1–3 years.

	1 year	2 years	3 years
Social / emotional	Demonstrates a range of emotions	Mainly parallel play	Some co-operative play
	Interested in watching peers	Emergence of pro-social behaviours such as empathy	Very curious
	Can be anxious in unfamiliar situations	Experiences strong emotions and has tantrums	Likes being given choices
	Plays in parallel	Can show defiance and expects needs to be met immediately	Needs clear boundaries for acceptable behaviour
	Shows affection and pleasure to familiar adults	Can be possessive with toys	Strong emotions and tantrums
			Enjoys learning routines and helping
Cognitive	Simple, goal-directed behaviour (e.g. moving towards a toy and then picking it up)	Begins to think symbolically	May begin to realise that other people have views that differ to their own
	Aware that a toy removed from play still exists	Starts to be able to predict behaviour of others from what they say (Wellman, 1990)	Can count up to three objects reliably
	Drops things to see what happens	Starts to engage in imaginary play and dressing up	
		Looks at story pictures to aid understanding	
Motor / physical	Crawling or bum-shuffling	Walking in a more controlled manner	Climbing
	May stand without support	Running around objects	Galloping
	Cruising	Jumping	Balancing
	Walking (with or without support)	Enjoys kicking and throwing (low level of competence)	Dancing
	Use of pincer movement to grab objects	Enjoys balance bikes or sit-'n'-ride toys	Jumping from raised heights
			May pedal a little on a bike

Table 2.1 Continued

	1 year	2 years	3 years
Communication / verbal	Babbling (repetitive, speech-like sounds)	May not speak very much yet	Vocabulary of two hundred words or more
	Some understanding of social cues (e.g. may say "hi" or wave to people who approach them)	Spoken vocabulary of around fifty words (can understand many more)	Using longer sentences to express ideas and desires
	Draws attention of carer to objects of interest with stares, utterances or pointing	Makes simple sentences	Chants, sings songs
	"Conversational" babbling	Understands simple directions (e.g. please close the door)	Displays curiosity through asking questions
	Different types of crying communicate anxiety, frustration, pain or tiredness.	Begins to recognise and sing rhymes	Can recite numbers
		Notices when they are being talked to and listens	Can be heard talking to self while playing
			Enjoys hearing favourite stories / rhymes again and again
Life skills	Can pick up small pieces of food and put into mouth, otherwise fed by spoon	Can use a spoon or fork to feed self	Potty trained
		Attempts to remove or put on items of clothing/shoes	May be using the toilet with help
		May be ready to potty train	Can put on/remove some items of clothing/shoes
			Can help tidy up
			May use knife and fork for eating

How young children learn

Research into how infants and children learn has been dominated by two twentieth-century giants: Piaget and Vygotsky. This dominance is largely justified; even though some aspects of their theories have been queried in the decades since publication, the main thrust of their arguments remain solid and compelling. John Dewey also contributed the theory of experiential learning to the debate. His ideas influenced teaching and learning for older children in schools and colleges, but are still relevant to us when working with young children.

We will look at these three key theories below, and see how they relate to our activity planning for an outdoor toddler group.

Jean Piaget

Although much is made of the differences between their theories, Piaget and Vygotsky both espoused a *constructivist* model of learning. They believed that children actively constructed their knowledge of the world around them by interacting with it, and used these concrete experiences to develop and refine their understanding. This was in stark contrast to previous theories of child development, in which infants and children were passive recipients of instruction and stimuli.

Piaget thought that babies and infants learn through developing and using *schemes*. A scheme is a set of thoughts, memories and actions which are all linked, and which can be used as a sort of template for how to achieve a goal.

New-born babies don't move much and, when they start, their limb movements seem quite random. As babies develop they begin to repeat certain movements or behaviours which brought satisfying results previously. This repetitive movement becomes a scheme. As their behaviour becomes more goal-directed, they combine smaller schemes to make larger ones, e.g. a scheme for grabbing an object with the one for shaking, to pick up and shake a toy.

When an existing scheme cannot be used to achieve the goal the infant has, for example their grabbing scheme does not work for a toy larger than their hand span, they adapt their existing template to accommodate this new experience, for example by trying to use both hands.

Thus, at all points during a child's development, their existing experience and understanding is brought to bear on a situation. If it doesn't work, the child attempts a different way to achieve their goal, which is then incorporated into their scheme. This process is called *accommodation*, and is what happens when we learn new skills or facts.

It is easy to see how, through a wide range of experiences with the surrounding world, children can expand their repertoire of interactions, outcomes and the schemes they use to navigate it, refining and combining them to achieve more complex and elaborate goals. Outdoor play gives infants and children the opportunity to practice and refine their schemes, e.g. pouring water or picking up stones and dropping them in a bucket to see what happens. This repetition allows them to make sense of what they are observing and internalise this new knowledge of how the world around them works. When children are investigating their ideas outside, the usual restrictions on mess, noise and space that they encounter when playing indoors are no longer a problem, giving them more freedom to pursue their ideas.

Lev Vygotsky

Vygotsky's ground-breaking theory was not published until the late 1970s, fifty years after Piaget's. Like Piaget, he viewed children as explorers on a quest to understand their environment, constructing their knowledge as they went. However, where Piaget viewed children as being engaged in solitary wanderings, Vygotsky stressed the importance of the social environment and interpersonal interaction in a child's learning and development. His theory filled some of the holes of Piagetian theory: if social interaction and the cultural environment has no role in development, then what explains the global developmental delay of children who have experienced chronic neglect?

In essence, Vygotsky thought that learning and development occurred first on the outside, from a social interaction such as a child asking their mum why we have to wear coats on a cold day, and then occurs on the inside, when the new knowledge is internalised.

He also posited a model for these interactions between children and key caregivers, called the *zone of proximal development*, or ZPD. This idea has been hugely influential on subsequent research into child development and education, because it looked at the supporting role which the adult can play in learning.

He defined the ZPD as "the difference between a child's actual developmental level . . . and their potential development . . . under adult guidance or collaboration with more capable peers." (Vygotsky, 1978: 86). Vygotsky felt that assessing the potential of a child to learn, with the adult tailoring their support to foster this potential, was far more valuable than just measuring what the child could already do independently. This was quite revolutionary because it shifted our measurement of ability from what a child can already do, such as play the recorder, which might be due to such socio-economic and cultural factors as wealthy parents and private lessons, to their potential to learn a new skill.

This in turn focused minds on the quality of the instruction being given to the child. Bruner (1983) expanded upon this with the concept of "scaffolding". This is where the adult supporting the child in their learning adjusts the amount of support and encouragement they are giving to the child as the child grapples with a new concept and then becomes more confident in using it independently. Initially, the support will be direct, such as giving specific commands, and may involve modelling so the child can copy. As the child develops their proficiency and confidence, the adult may scaffold them in indirect ways, such as hinting what they might want to consider or suggesting ways to streamline the process or improve the outcome.

The sociocultural model of learning is still very influential today and leaders are taught about scaffolding as a key strategy for effective classroom learning. For people working with a much younger age range, scaffolding is still relevant because it shows how important social interaction is for babies and young children, and how the quality of interaction from primary caregivers can affect a child's development. It shows us the value of supporting a child's attempts to do something for themselves, such as putting on their wellies, as opposed to just doing it for them because they can't do it yet. It highlights the importance of choosing activities for our groups which the children can attempt in a way which would be satisfying to them. It also shows us the value to the child of having those endless "why . . .?" questions answered!

John Dewey

Dewey's contribution to this field of interest was the concept of experiential learning (also referred to as accelerated learning). As mentioned earlier, this idea has had a huge impact on education from nursery to university, and is based on the idea that learning through first-hand experience of something is deeper and more meaningful to the individual. Thus, a child who plays on a seesaw has a much clearer, first-hand experience of what it was like and how to make a seesaw work than a child who watched them playing, or another who saw a seesaw in a picture.

For us, the theory of experiential learning provides a rationale for exploratory play outside, as young children make meaning from their surroundings through interacting with it: touching, pulling, putting, dropping, pushing, scraping, pouring, dragging, stroking, waving, tossing, rolling, scattering, filling . . . . The list is as endless as their curiosity.

The role of play in learning

At the simplest level, play allows a baby to develop its schemes for moving different parts of its body, as it gradually begins to exercise more control over its movements.

It also allows babies to explore interesting objects by manipulating and investigating them to explore textures, colours, tastes, sounds and smells. This exploration often involves putting them in their mouth. The movement involved in play – picking, placing, stacking, dropping, selecting – also allows the developing child to practice and refine their gross and fine motor movements while learning about how things work.

As babies become more mobile and grow into toddlers, they are able to investigate more of their surroundings, and attempt to manipulate them by seeing what happens when they drop, tug, push or pull the things they find, as any new parent child-proofing their cupboards will know.

As young children recognise what some toys represent, e.g. a toy car, they can use them to reinforce what they already understand about them in real life, such as making them move along the floor or making noises to imitate the engine's roar. They practice what they have learned from watching adults, such as playing with pots and pans to pretend to cook.

As they get older, they start to play symbolically. This means that an object with a known purpose, such as a stick, is used to as a broom to sweep the floor.

Children can also rehearse the rules and behaviours that they have seen around them by engaging in pretend play. An example of this is playing shops or mums and dads.

How this relates to your activity planning

You may be feeling a little confused by now. On the one hand, the evidence points to the benefits to child development of exploring and actively testing out their existing ideas. On the other, we've got the role of the carer in scaffolding the child's understanding so that they can do things which they couldn't do on their own. At what point do we just sit back and let them play? Or should we be constantly hovering in the background, ready to help?

The pejorative term "helicopter parent" has been recently coined to describe parents who are so busy protecting their child's interests that they are inhibiting their child's development as an independent thinker who can stand on their own two feet. How can we ensure that we don't give with one hand and take away with the other?

The simple answer is that children need a mix: a mix of activities which allow free exploration and more guided activity. This way, they are free to pursue their fascinations but also gain more ideas and information to make sense of their world.

When planning your sessions, include time for free play and structured activity.

Another key point to take from all this research into child development is that there is a wide gap between the life experience and development of a one year old and a three year old, so you will need to cater for both ends of the spectrum. (Even if you have a group of children who were all born in the same year, the January births are almost one year older than the December births.) For your youngest children, you may need to provide a smaller, safe area for sensory exploration from where they can watch the older children. Your older, more mobile children will need a wider area to roam around and will want to be active – running, fetching, carrying, pouring, talking, hiding, making and jumping.

A final point is the important role that adults can play in scaffolding the learning of children. Learning is a shared process and the support of a trusted adult will make it more effective (Department for Education, 2005). If you're setting up a toddler group and are wondering about whether to make it a "parent and toddler" one where the parent stays, the obvious advantage is that each child will have their own trusted helper. If you are working within an established nursery or childcare setting, you will already have ratios of adult carers to children to adhere to.

Typical behaviours and what they might mean

If you already work with young children or have some of your own, forgive me for stating the obvious below. If you are new to the field of working with little ones, however, it's important to be aware of some of the common behavioural and organisational characteristics of working with this age range. I have necessarily focused on the more confusing aspects, but let's not forget that working with children is fun and richly rewarding.

They won't talk to you

Don't take this personally! The children you work with may take some time to become familiar with you, to trust you and to smile at you or talk. They might turn their heads away, look to their carer for cuddles or even look like they're going to cry when you approach them. It's a sign of healthy attachment to their primary caregivers, and given time, they will warm to you.

What to do about it: understand that anxiety in unfamiliar social situations and clinginess are developmental stages that all children pass through. Crouch down to meet their height, talk kindly and smile. If they turn away or seem anxious, don't try to push them into communicating with you, just politely move on. When giving instructions, sit in a circle so they can watch as well as listen, and keep it simple.

Tantrums

With the best planning, kindest helpers and nicest resources in the world, you will sometimes find yourself dealing with an agitated or angry child who is having a temper tantrum. If you find this an unsettling experience, it is worth remembering that tantrums are developmental stage that most children pass through as they learn to regulate their feelings and urges.

What to do about it: the advantage of having parents or carers in attendance here is obvious; they deal with the behavioural issues that sometimes arise while you work with the rest of the group.

If parents are not present and you can establish that the tantrum was due to a something like taking turns, encourage the children to play fairly and praise them when they do so. If there is no clear reason, distraction is one of the best ways of dealing with a tantrum. "Would you like to help me collect the buckets?" or "Have you ever seen one of these before [show item and then let the child touch it]?" are ways of distracting the child and engaging them in another activity. You can also walk them away from the place where they became upset, while talking to them about something else.

To ensure that you treat all children consistently and fairly, decide in advance how you want to deal with challenging or difficult behaviours in your Behaviour Management procedure and ensure that all practitioners and helpers working with you have read it and understand it (see Chapter 5).

Short attention spans . . .

Young children have very short attention spans and can move through whatever activity you have planned very quickly. It is not uncommon for a toddler to give something a quick try before wanting to return to what they were doing earlier.

What to do about it: don't be disheartened by this – once again, it's a reflection of their developmental stage. However, make sure your activities are easy for them to follow and join in with, and always have some extra games up your sleeve (see Chapter 8: Activity bank). It's fine for the children to break off and explore the site every now and then, as long as they are accompanied by their parent or another practitioner is looking out for them.

. . . And obsessions

The inverse of the above is also true! It is quite characteristic of young children to become gripped by a particular aspect of how something works and to want to explore that endlessly. This means that they won't participate in the rest of the activities because they are still doing it . . . and still doing it . . .

What you can do about it: relax. It doesn't matter whether they're following what you're doing or not, as long as they're happily engaged and playing safely with a parent or practitioner keeping an eye them. This is typical behaviour of young children, and if you don't get to cover all the activities you had planned because they're all obsessed with the watering cans today, it doesn't matter. They're still having fun and learning!

They won't sit still and listen

Of course they won't! That doesn't come for years. Children of that age are egocentric in that they are aware of their own interests and ideas and keen to pursue them, and blissfully unaware of the social rules and etiquette that we take for granted. During any activity, some children will join in and others will be picking their nose, wandering around, refusing to do anything, asking whether they can play with the watering cans yet or talking loudly about their cat.

What you can do about it: again, relax. This is par for the course. However, you can increase their ability to engage with what you're doing by speaking clearly and simply. Make any instructions brief, demonstrating what you mean so that they can see as well as hear what they are going to do. Don't forget that the adults present will also be listening, so they will be able to help the children who were focused on other things during your input.

They don't seem to understand

This is quite reasonable. You are a brand new person to them, with a new way of talking, moving and being. They might need to spend some time just staring at you and sussing you out before they can concentrate on what you're trying to say!

What you can do about it: respect the fact that it will take them some time to understand you. Speak clearly and kindly at all times. Give simple explanations and always model the activities they are about to participate in. And perhaps most importantly, smile! Smile a lot. It fosters trust and feels nicer for all of you.

They won't do anything

You may encounter a child who does not want to join in with any of the activities, and instead just watches the other children playing.

What you can do about it: bear in mind that this is something that some children do when they are getting used to new situations – they stand back and observe before joining in. As long as the child is not distressed, let them watch and approach every so often with some of the equipment you're using, e.g. a bucket and spade, to see if they would like to play with one. They will join in when they feel comfortable.

3 Getting your site ready

In this chapter we will look at:

- what to look for and look out for when choosing a site;
- some types of places to consider;
- preparing for a meeting with the site owner/representative;
- site preparation: clearing things up before putting things in;
- activity zoning: how it works and how to do it.

What kind of thing am I looking for?

When you are looking at possible sites, choose somewhere with some or all of the following:

- ground partially or completely covered in grass;
- enclosed by a combination of gates/hedges/walls/fences;
- some trees or bushes to provide shade and interest;
- a good supply of natural materials to use, e.g. leaves from surrounding shrubs and trees, grass cuttings, weeds, stones, sticks;
- large enough to accommodate activities for infants and toddlers simultaneously;
- easy access to toilets and wash basins;
- parking nearby (if parents have to bring their child to the site);
- safe pedestrian access to the site (if not using existing childcare setting).

Don't worry if your site is an irregular shape; if the site is enclosed these kinds of places can be ideal for activity zoning (see below). It's also fine if the ground in your site is undulating or uneven; uneven terrain is much better for developing a child's motor skills and spatial awareness. It's also more fun to explore!

Things to consider

Access to toilets

You don't *have* to provide access to toilets during your session, but it will obviously be better for everyone attending if you do. Some parents will not want to change their child's nappy under a tree, however nice the scenery is, and some children will be uncomfortable about popping behind a bush to answer the call of nature, as will some of the adults. If you choose a site with no toilets nearby, make sure that this is made completely clear to the parents and carers before they book.

If you do have toilets on site, such as a community centre or scout hut, you will need to make sure that you have the key to unlock the main building. Put down something to protect the floor from muddy footprints, such as newspaper, lino or cut and flattened cardboard boxes – this will save you a mopping job when you pack up later. Give the walls a quick wipe for muddy handprints before you leave, and check with the site representative if they want you to empty the toilet bin or leave it for the cleaner, as it will probably have a couple of soiled nappies in it by the end of the session.

Storage

A site with limited storage facilities or none at all can still be used, but you will need to use your own garage or car boot to compensate. Check whether you can leave specific resources and equipment on site, or locked up in the main building with the site representative. Different kinds of storage are described in more detail in Chapter 4.

Hazards

Avoid choosing a site with any of the following:

* a pond – toddlers and babies can drown in shallow water if they fall or crawl in;
* gaps in the fence or hedge which give children unsupervised access to the road outside;
* concealed parts of the site to which the general public also have access;
* no clear boundaries along most edges, such as walls, fences or hedgerows;
* ant hills.

It is important to consider boundaries for your site. If the land the other side of the "boundary" looks identical to where they were playing, e.g. more trees and grass – they will become quickly disorientated. A child who is lost doesn't know how to find their way back again, and you must avoid putting them at risk of becoming so. If the site you are considering has no clear boundary, I would strongly advise you to find somewhere else.

Possible sites

The more you look, the more possibilities you will see for somewhere to use, but below is a list of starting points in your local community. Often these facilities are unused during the day and have some grounds attached. A key advantage to these kinds of places is that you have access to toilets and washing facilities. They are also easy for local parents to find, and to reach on foot or by bus.

- W.I. hall
- church hall
- community centre
- family or children's centre
- library (NB: may not be able to provide access to toilets)
- scout or guide hut
- village hall
- local park or community garden
- city farm.

You might find that the grounds you can use are a bit plain – grassy with a border of shrubs and trees or fence – but you can develop the site into a more varied and exciting place to explore by using some of the ideas further on in this chapter.

If you want somewhere that feels a bit wilder, you could try the following options by looking online for areas local to you:

- local nature reserve
- Woodland Trust reserves
- Wildlife Trust community reserves
- Green Flag nature reserves
- community farms
- farmers with land to rent out for activities
- National Trust (some properties will hire part of their grounds for regular activities for children).

Bear in mind that using such sites may limit access to those with their own transport, and you will need to ensure that there is adequate parking nearby. They are also less likely to have toilets and hand-washing facilities, although natural materials should be available in abundance!

These kinds of places will give unrestricted access to the rest of the general population while your group is running. You will need to be aware of strangers coming and going, people walking their dogs, and have agreed a procedure for keeping the children in your group safe in the event of unwanted advances by either.

Existing childcare settings

If you are expanding the outdoor provision of an existing nursery or childcare setting, you will need to look at your existing outdoor area and how it is currently used. You may decide to revamp and improve what you have to create more natural spaces for exploratory and creative play. Some links for ideas about how to develop the site are given in Chapter 9. On the other hand, you may feel that will have a negative impact on other types of outdoor activity, such as cycling, scooting, climbing and running.

If you do not think it possible to provide the opportunity for creative outdoor play at your existing site, you might want to consider finding another site nearby which could be used. You will need to decide on how the children will be safely transported to and from the site – walking crocodile, minibus – and notify parents of the plans, per setting policy.

Collection of children from another site

If you decide to run a group at a different site to your setting and have the parents come and collect their children, you will need to ensure that:

- Parents and carers are **all aware** of this arrangement, have consented to their child participating and have been given clear directions of how to find it.
- All staff running the group are aware of any restrictions on who collects the children, e.g. parents who have been prevented by court order from contact.
- You have a clear policy, agreed in advance, of what to do if a parent does not turn up on time.

Preparing for a meeting with the site representative

Let's assume that you have found what looks like an ideal venue for your group, and you need to seek permission to use it from the site owner or site representative.

21

Making a good impression

When you're getting ready to ask a stranger to do you a favour, making a good first – and second – impression is critical. People are far more likely to grant favours or respond positively to someone who turns up on time, knows what they're talking about and looks as though they can be relied upon to do what they said they would. You don't need to roll up in a business suit with a brolly and briefcase, but you do need to come across as organised and trustworthy.

Preparing for the meeting will put you at ease and make it easier for them to understand what you want to do. You might also find it useful to have someone else accompany you to the meeting, to take notes while you talk. (If you do this, make sure that you're both in agreement about the purpose of the meeting and what you're asking for – it will be quite baffling for the site representative if you both say something different!)

Below is a guide to the meeting process:

To arrange an initial meeting:

- Find out who you need to talk to at the organisation.
- Phone or email this person to introduce yourself, briefly introduce your idea for a group and organise a face-to-face meeting.
- If you send a letter, bear in mind that you will need to follow this up with a phone-call to arrange a meeting.

Preparing for the meeting:

- Produce a short document which states the following: what the group is; where you propose it will meet; when you will meet and for how long; typical activities; any access requirements your group will have to facilities such as toilets; assumptions you have made about how you will use the proposed site; storage of equipment; safety and roles and responsibilities, e.g. who is responsible for keeping the brambles cut back, where you will get the key for the main building from.
- Print off copies for yourself and anyone else attending the meeting to read (you may wish to post a copy in advance, but still bring a paper copy in case they have lost theirs).
- Plan to arrive fifteen minutes early.
- Make sure that you have a number written down that you can call if you are unavoidably delayed.
- If you can, find out if there are already activities taking place on the site which are similar to your plans.

At the meeting:

- Find out if there is a charge for using the land, and if so how much it is.
- Be honest about whether you want to charge money to those attending your group – some site representatives may be willing to charge you less if you aren't making a profit.
- Go through your document (this will only be a side or two of A4) and see if they have any questions or comments.
- Note down their comments as you go (a pen or pencil is fine for this – you can type it up later) and any actions agreed.
- Be respectful of their time and keep the meeting to half an hour or so.
- Offer to send a summary of what was agreed during the meeting and check if they would prefer to receive it by email or letter.

After the meeting:

- Send a summary of what was discussed and agreed within the next 48 hours – being prompt and reliable will reinforce their positive impressions from the meeting.
- Include: who is doing what, by which date, where/why and any issues still unresolved and actions to be taken to resolve them.
- Ask them to read the summary and come back to you with comments or questions by a certain date.
- If appropriate suggest a future date for a further meeting to resolve any outstanding issues.

Once everything is sorted out, keep in touch with your contact to find out about issues which might affect you and keep them abreast of any changes you might be planning. Be prepared to discuss the roles and responsibilities of maintaining the site and access to it, to ensure that you all agree and understand – this will prevent minor misunderstandings becoming diplomatic incidents. And another obvious point, but one worth making: leave the site as you found it when you have finished. Clear away all your resources, per agreement, and pick up any litter which has found its way onto the site, even if your group did not drop it.

Bear in mind that some people will welcome you and your group with open arms, and others might be more wary. Try not to take this personally; they may have had their fingers burned before, or heard a horror story about an incompetent group leader from a colleague. Be professional and patient, and with time you will build familiarity and trust with them.

> ## Local authority areas – do you need a permit?
>
> Some local authorities have a permits system for using parks and other recreational areas. These permits will give you permission to run your group without being fined. It's worth checking whether the issuing office keeps some kind of "activity diary" to prevent half a dozen personal trainers and group leaders all descending at the same time, however!

Preparing the site

Once your site is confirmed, you will be itching to prepare it. If you want to keep as much greenery and shade as possible, it can be hard to know what you should leave alone and what you should try and remove or cut back. The ideas below can serve as an initial guide, but before embarking on any gardening or clearing activity, check with the site representative or owner that they are happy for you to do so.

What to clear back, and what to leave

Weeds: leave these to flower and grow all year round because they will provide excellent resources to use. The only circumstances under which you might want to clear them back would be if they are blocking access to and from the site, or seriously encroaching on the open space. If you're using a nature reserve or similar, check with the site representative about rare species which should not be picked, and ensure that the adults attending all know to prevent the children from picking them.

Brambles: given that the children in your group may be crawling and doing lots of exploring at ground level, cut back any tough and prickly bramble bushes which are spreading out of the hedgerows and taking over the rest of the plants in the zone you think you will be using for infants. You can also encourage the growth of other kinds of weeds and creeping shrubs by cutting back the brambles. (If you want to try and stop a bramble bush growing at all, you will need to cut it back right down to the ground, and keep trimming off any new growth. These plants are very determined!) Dispose of the cuttings offsite or burn them.

Nettles: although these can sting small hands, they are also excellent for attracting insects, so bear this in mind when cutting them back. As a rule of thumb, cut back any overgrown areas to give more space for the children to play safely, and then keep an eye on the regrowth.

Toadstools or other fungi: if you find that you have some growing at ground level on your site, you will need to show the parents/carers exactly where they are, so that they can prevent their children from picking or ingesting them. If you don't think that this will work, cover them with crates and a blanket draped over the top and assign an adult to ensure that they are not found. Alternatively, start looking for another site.

Making a site plan

A site plan is a very simple sketch of the shape of your site and the features within it. You can do one of these on a sheet of plain A4 paper. The purpose of a site plan is to familiarise you with the layout of the site and the location of trees, fences, walls, steps, etc. so that you can better plan your activities and avoid accidents.

To make a site plan, all you need is a sheet of A4 paper, a clipboard to lean on, and a pencil. Walk around the site a couple of times to get the shape of its boundary fixed in your head, and then sketch the boundary on your sheet. Then add such features as: trees, bushes, hedgerows, gates, steps, access points to and from site, nettle beds, bramble bushes, sloping ground and any other features. You can add these features using simple circles or crosses. Try and keep the space between them on your site plan roughly similar to the way that they appear on the site.

When finished, make a several copies of it and then you can use one as a planning aid each time you are creating activity zones.

Activity zoning

Activity zoning is a way of designating different areas in your site to different activities.

Why use activity zoning?

Using activity zoning:

- ensures whole site is being used during the session;
- protects areas for children of different ages and their developmental needs;
- encourages a child's exploration of the whole site over time;
- provides sheltered areas for infants and space for more physical activities for older children during the same session;
- makes planning easy for staff: who is setting up, supervising and clearing up each activity;
- makes a plain-looking site more enticing and exciting.

Would I have to use activity zoning all the time?

No. Depending on the size of your site and the type of group you are running – such as one with one leader and all the children doing the same activity – you may decide that it is not suitable. If this is the case, please refer to Chapter 8 for a bank of activity ideas and guidance on planning your sessions.

However, if you want to run sessions with activities which children can join in with as they wish – such as a drop-in group – activity zoning is essential to ensure that all the activities have sufficient space, a balanced range of activities to suit different ages is offered and your staff know what they're doing. Consider screening off an area which is only used by infants when planning your activity zones. More details about each type of plan can be found in Chapter 7.

Ideas for activity zones

If you think that activity zoning is going to work well for your group, consider adopting four or five zones per session. The beauty of this model is that you can change them from week to week, depending on what resources you come across and the changing seasons. This is by no means an exhaustive list; you can add more as you think of them!

- quiet area
- water play
- digging and planting
- den-making
- hiding and camouflage
- climbing, e.g. trees or "obstacle course"
- active games, e.g. balls, skittles, bean bags, hoops, running
- craft area
- imaginative play
- painting zone
- mud kitchen
- group games, e.g. "Grandmother's Footsteps", "What's the Time, Mr. Wolf?"

How can I create activity zones?

This is where your site plan comes in useful! Take a copy and mark out where the activities will run, based on the natural features of the site. For example, a sloping area, trees or shrubs, low walls or tree trunks or a picnic table could all be used to separate activity areas.

If your site doesn't have any of these, you can easily create some boundaries with the following:

- a sheet or blanket hung over a rope tied to two uprights
- a play tunnel
- a plank laid on the ground
- a couple of large potted plants placed next to each other
- a trellis panel or fence panel propped up securely between some rocks or bricks
- crates made into a low wall for the children to look through, or draped with an old curtain to add some colour
- logs laid across the ground to show the boundary
- chalk marks (this will work on a hard surface)
- a short rope laid along the ground to divide areas (ensure that the children do not get tangled up in it).

It goes without saying that anything you use on your site will have been checked carefully by you or someone else in your team for sharp edges and general sturdiness. Avoid using tent pegs to secure anything, because young children will tread on or trip over them.

How to develop your site over time

As your group settles in to their outdoor toddler group site, you will start to notice different ways in which you could enhance it. Your ideas will be restricted by the type of site you have found, who owns it and who else uses it, but below are some pointers to get you started:

Attracting wildlife

- minibeast piles made from rotting wood and dead leaves
- bird table
- insect hotels
- hanging squirrel nuts from trees
- bird boxes and feeding tables
- planting wild flower seeds to attract butterflies, ladybirds and bees.

Developing boundaries for activity zoning

- Plant a line of shrubs, or use large pots if you need to remove them after the session.
- Create a willow structure to screen off a particular area (this is done by planting a row of willow whips and then "weaving" them together to create a tunnel or archway).

27

- Put in a trellis and plant vines to cover it.
- Build a low wall from large stones or painted breezeblocks.
- Make a wattle and daub wall – the children can help with this!

Shelter and storage

- Fix wooden battens to a wall so that you can fix an awning there as a shelter from the weather.
- Build a permanent sheltered seating area.
- Buy a shed for storing equipment.

Fruit, blossoms, foliage and flowers

- Plant apple, cherry or pear trees.
- Create a strawberry patch.
- Plant plenty of Spring bulbs (these can either be planted in the ground or in pots which you can place around the site and then move out of the way afterwards).
- Choose sun-loving or shade-loving plants to add more foliage and variety to blank corners of your site.

Sensory garden

- Find four or five different types of plants that have pungent aromas and plant them in pots or a flowerbed.

For more detailed guidance on how to implement these ideas, look at the links in Chapter 9 or search online. Alternatively, Sally Featherstone's *Little Book of Outdoor Play* (2001) has some excellent guidance on choosing plants and flowers for different conditions and purposes.

4 | What will I need?

In this chapter we will look at:

- where to find resources;
- suggestions for resource collections and storage;
- record-keeping requirements;
- first aid and insurance requirements;
- qualifications for you and anyone you employ;
- tax affairs you may need to consider.

Please note: this chapter focuses entirely on resources for activities. It should be read in conjunction with Chapter 5 which offers advice on what safety equipment is also required for your group.

Finding resources

The first question is: where do I get them from? And especially on a limited budget? And the answer is: anywhere and everywhere! Your garage, the charity shop, a local scrap store or recycling centre, specialist stockists, pound shops, budget supermarkets . . . . The only limiting factor will be whether the thing you're considering can be used safely by small children.

When building up your resource collection, also consider the "bash factor": a small paint brush will take a lot less wear and tear from regular use by young children than a large paintbrush for use with emulsion paint or a paint roller will. Before you add something to your collection, consider whether it will still be in one piece at the end of some vigorous use!

Exactly what you need will depend on what type of group you are running, and where. Those of you in more wooded environments might want to focus more on the use of natural materials, den-building, digging, mud kitchen and exploration games. Those of you in an area which has less natural cover or natural materials to use might decide you need to lay on more art and craft or water activities to provide interest.

Safety first

Check all resources for their suitability, rejecting any which have sharp edges, exposed nails, rust, hinges which could trap small fingers, flaking paint or splinters. Obviously, do not use anything made of glass.

Resource collections

If using activity zoning, you might find it useful to create your own resource lists, based on your zones. Alternatively, you might want to plan your activities by theme or based on story-books (see Chapter 8). These lists are intended as a starting point but are neither essential or exhaustive; add your own ideas, pick and choose what suits your interests and your setting.

Art/painting:

- large brushes for painting walls, rollers, wallpaper paste brushes
- plastic mixing trays or large palettes
- buckets
- stiff card/cut-up cardboard boxes
- old rolls of wallpaper for whole-group pictures
- pens, crayons
- chalk (get the jumbo size pieces because they are easier for small hands to hold and don't snap as easily)
- ready-mixed paint
- water pots (these can be large yoghurt pots).

Water play:

- paddling pool
- buckets
- pots, containers, jugs, spoons, cups

- bubble-blowing equipment
- watering cans (child-sized)
- floating toys such as ducks, boats, balls
- funnels
- squeezy bottles, such as washing up liquid, washed out thoroughly
- spray bottles, such as old cleaning sprays, cleaned and rinsed out thoroughly
- ice cubes
- food colouring and detergent to add to the water.

Environmental:

- magnifying glasses (plastic)
- spades, trowels (child-sized)
- plant pots of different sizes and colours
- minibeast piles
- insect hotel
- rocks
- shells
- pebbles
- logs
- tree stumps
- stepping stones made from thick slices of a cut tree trunk
- bag of compost (if the children cannot dig up soil on site)
- wheelbarrow (child-sized).

Outdoor gym:

- ropes (for laying trails to follow and marking boundaries on the ground)
- hoops (can lay on the ground or suspend from trees)
- beanbags/soft balls
- planks (checked carefully for splinters and sharp edges) and an A-frame
- plastic crates
- large cardboard boxes with the base and top opened so they can be crawled through
- targets for suspending from trees/fastening to wall
- play tunnel.

Mud kitchen:

- metal pots and pans
- old wooden spoons or large metal spoons
- jug or old squash bottle for water
- old oven trays and dishes, checked carefully for safety
- shelf for putting pots and trays on (this can be an old cupboard, or a tree trunk lying on the ground).

Den building:

- branches, twigs and leaves
- logs
- tree stumps
- blankets or large towels
- sheets or curtains
- old climbing frames, checked for safety
- washing airers
- plastic crates
- old cushions
- ropes (to tie between two uprights and drape a sheet over)
- old garden furniture, child-sized and checked for safety.

Role-play corner:

- rubber dinghy
- tent
- picnic set and blanket
- café (a crate or box with a table cloth over it and some tree stumps or cushions for seats)
- paddling pool (always have a practitioner present to supervise a filled paddling pool)
- hammock
- garden centre with plant pots, trowels, spades and soil.

Contributions from parents and helpers:

It's always wise to have a list of resources you need for upcoming activities, so that parents and other staff can contribute. Ideas to start with would be:

- toilet roll and kitchen roll tubes
- squeezy bottles, e.g. washing up liquid
- spray bottles, e.g. anti-bacterial spray
- old saucepans
- old tea towels, curtains, sheets, blankets and cushions
- clear plastic bottles with lids
- egg boxes
- planting trays from the garden centre
- large corrugated cardboard boxes
- old outdoor toys and equipment, such as hoops, plastic balls, skipping ropes.

Storage

You will need a range of storage options. The simplest is large plastic boxes with lids which can be bought at the pound shop or supermarket, and smaller, clean plastic food containers. Depending on your arrangement with the site representative, you might be allowed to store some or all of your equipment on site or inside the building. If not, try one or more of the following ideas:

- shed (check if you need permission to erect one)
- mini greenhouse (these are very cheap to buy and will protect equipment from the rain)
- plastic chest of drawers
- trolley
- garage
- the boot of your car!

Record-keeping

The type of records you need to keep will depend on whether you are charging for the group or not. As a minimum you will need the contact information suggested below.

Contact information

If you are working within an established childcare setting, you should already have this. If you are setting the group up from scratch, you will need to collect the following information from parents when they book a place for their child:

The child:

- name
- date of birth, so you can work out age in years and months
- any known allergies
- any known emergency medication, e.g. inhaler, epipen
- mobility (crawling/cruising/walking/running)
- communication (babbling/few words/short sentences/speech)
- any other special requirements (partially sighted, deafness, etc.).

The parent or carer:

- name
- relationship to child
- contact number (a mobile number is best, so that you can text or call in the event of a sudden cancellation)
- email address (you can use this for sending the Information Sheet and Joining Letter mentioned in Chapter 6, saving money on postage)
- postal address (if you need to post receipts for payment).

Payment records

Site rent

If you are paying to use the site, you will need to keep the following:

- A record of how much has been paid, the time period covered, and the date by which the next payment is required.
- Receipts for payment received by the site representative.

Equipment and resources

For all kinds of groups, you will need to keep receipts for any purchases of resources or equipment. These will be useful just for keeping track of what has been spent from your budget, but if you are self-employed they can also be listed as business expenses against your tax assessment. For more information see the HMRC website listed in Chapter 9.

Charging for attendance

If you are charging for the group, you will need to keep the following records:

- The total number of parents and children attending and the total amount taken per session.
- If you are booking children in blocks, for example of four sessions paid for up front, you will need the date their payment was received and the date upon which they need to rebook.

Insurance

If you are running your group for an existing childcare setting, you may already be covered by their policies. Check them carefully, especially if you are not a regular employee of the company, or if you are taking the children off-site.

If you are setting up your group from scratch, check your insurance requirements with the site representative and an insurance company which specialises in covering childcare settings. It's likely that you will need to take out personal liability insurance. This typically lasts for a year before needing renewal. If you have employees working with you, make sure you ask if they are covered by the policy too.

Whatever you do, don't decide to wing it. If someone has an accident during one of your sessions and you have nothing to cover you it could prove costly, time-consuming and ruinous to your reputation and business.

First aid

You will need a member of staff to be a qualified paediatric first aider. This is very easy to sort out – St John's Ambulance run two-day, Ofsted-approved, first aid courses for staff working in early years settings. If you are going to have a large group you will need to check the guidance in the Early Years Framework to make sure you have the correct number of first aiders to children. If you are planning on running your group somewhere fairly remote, you will need training in paediatric first aid outdoors from an accredited provider. You will also need an extra adult working with you at all sessions so that they can meet the emergency services while you administer first aid. Some links for organisations providing this training are given in Chapter 9.

What qualifications will I need?

This depends on which type of group you are running.

Existing childcare setting: you will need the minimum qualifications required by your employer for working with this age range. Your DBS check will also need to be in date.

You will need to check whether you are covered by the insurance the setting currently holds for what you want to do.

Parents stay for the session: you will need to hold a paediatric first aid certificate and have a clean DBS check. Anyone else working with you, whether voluntary or paid, will need to hold a clean DBS check. All staff will need to be covered by personal liability insurance.

Parents drop off their children: you will need to hold minimum childcare qualifications for working with this age range, a paediatric first aid certificate and clean DBS check. Anyone else working with you, whether on a voluntary or paid basis, will need to hold minimum childcare qualifications for working with this age range and a clean DBS check. All staff will need to be covered by personal liability insurance.

Please note that although these requirements were correct at the time of writing, you should check to ensure that they are still accurate.

Tax affairs

This section is relevant if:

- You are self-employed and using the profits from your group as a source of income.
- You are thinking of setting up a business for running the group, either on your own or with other people working for you.

Local tax offices run regular "tax workshops" for people setting up a business. These workshops are free to attend and useful; a tax expert employed by Her Majesty's Revenues and Customs (HMRC) will explain the rules and requirements and answer any questions you have about working as a sole trader or employing others.

Your earnings from the group will need to be declared, along with records of any costs that you have incurred through purchasing equipment and resources for use by the group. If you are not yet registered, you will need to visit the HMRC website and follow the advice given on how to register.

Whatever your plans, if you are going to make some income from the group you must ensure that you are working within the law – visit the website, attend one of the local tax workshops and get informed.

5 Staying safe and having fun

In this chapter we will look at:

- what clothing you and the children will need;
- safety considerations for going out in all kinds of weathers;
- providing shelter from the elements;
- adult-to-child ratios;
- site boundaries;
- doing a risk assessment;
- accidents, emergencies and evacuation procedures.

Going out in all weathers

As previously discussed, children benefit from experiencing the outdoors throughout the year. Our climate brings us plenty of sunshine, but also rain, wind and snow. Dressing appropriately for the weather is key to running a good group; after all, how will you inspire the children if you are shivering and damp? Keeping yourself warm and dry, or cool and well hydrated, is important because you will be on site before the children arrive and still there tidying up after they leave.

What you need

Cold or rainy weather

- Waterproof trousers and a waterproof coat
- walking boots or wellies (bear in mind that your feet will get colder quicker in wellies and wear extra or thicker socks)

- wool or fleece hat
- gloves or fingerless gloves
- fleece or warm jumper
- long-sleeved top
- trousers
- scarf.

Simple waterproof coat and trouser sets can be bought cheaply from outdoor stockists. Another good place to try is budget supermarkets, which tend to stock outdoor clothing at different times during the year. If your budget allows, splash out on ski or snowboarding wear, which is very warm as well as waterproof.

Hot and sunny weather

- Factor 50 sunblock
- a hat or cap
- sunglasses
- loose-fitting top which covers your shoulders, back and chest
- comfortable trousers
- a long-sleeved top
- waterproofs
- plenty of drinking water.

The main thing to remember when it's hot and sunny is this: don't be tempted to use it as a chance to work on your tan. As stated before, you'll be in the glare of the sun for much longer than everyone else, setting things up and tidying away after, and at a much greater risk of getting painful sunburn. Cover your exposed skin with sunblock and reapply as often as you think appropriate. A long-sleeved top is always useful for when the sun goes in and it's suddenly very cold, and waterproofs are always there in case it starts to rain! Trousers are better than shorts for the protection they offer against scrapes, scratches and sunburn, but it's up to you. Sunglasses are not essential, but can be useful.

Other essentials

- Wet wipes
- antibacterial hand gel
- first aid kit

- fully charged mobile phone
- something for you to eat and drink.

Wet wipes and antibacterial gel are always useful for cleaning hands, even if there are sinks nearby. It goes without saying that you will need to bring a first aid kit, as discussed further on in this chapter. Unless you are running the group at an existing childcare setting, you will also need a fully charged mobile phone for making emergency calls. And don't forget your own needs: keep your energy levels up and stay well-hydrated by bringing a snack and a drink with you.

What the children need to bring

If parents are attending, you can provide them with a list of what they need to bring with them in their Joining Letter (see Chapter 6). If you are running your group through an existing childcare setting, you may choose to provide the gear or ask for parents to help out.

It's worth pointing out that although the parent is responsible for dressing their child appropriately, you – as the group leader – are responsible for advising them on suitable clothing. There are plenty of families who don't play outdoors for long periods of time unless it's a nice day, so they won't necessarily know what to bring.

Cold or wet weather

- Snowsuit or warm, waterproof coat and trousers
- trousers or tights, vest and jumper underneath
- wellies and thick socks
- mittens
- fleecy or woolly hat
- whatever drinks and snacks the parent feels their child will need.

Hot and sunny weather

- Factor 50 sunblock
- a sun hat or cap
- clothes that cover the child's body, legs and shoulders
- a cardigan or long-sleeved top to slip on if it gets cold
- waterproofs – because you never know!
- plenty of drinking water.

Carrying spares

If you are running a group in a deprived area, you will probably want to get a stock of spare wellies, child-size waterproofs and coats so that children without these at home can participate. Charity shops, car boot sales and school jumble sales are great places to pick things up cheaply. Alternatively, send a note round at work asking for any children's outdoor gear which has been outgrown.

Dealing with extremes

Dressing appropriately is a major part of avoiding problems such as hypothermia or heatstroke. I would like to stress the rarity of these conditions, but you must always bear in mind that exposure to extreme heat or cold can cause these. Each child's threshold will be different, depending on underlying factors such as general health, tiredness, medical conditions and diet. Children under the age of two are particularly vulnerable.

Here are some simple guidelines for spotting the symptoms, and also preventing the situation from arising in the first place.

Hypothermia

Hypothermia occurs when the body's core temperature drops, due to the person becoming excessively cold.

Causes:

- being under-dressed for the weather;
- remaining inactive outdoors for long periods of time;
- staying outside for too long and becoming dangerously cold;
- wearing clothes in the cold that have become soaked through with water.

Symptoms:

- constant shivering
- tiredness
- looking pale
- cold skin
- fast breathing
- confusion, poor co-ordination and peculiar behaviour.

Treatment:

Someone with mild to moderate hypothermia may not necessarily display all of the symptoms described above. If you have any concerns at all:

- call the emergency services straight away;
- settle the child in a sheltered place, indoors if possible, with another adult to support them and monitor their condition;
- wrap them up in an extra layer such as a blanket.

How to avoid it in the first place:

- on very cold, wet or windy days, only allow children who are dressed appropriately to participate;
- shorten the length of the session, e.g. from one hour to forty-five minutes, or forty minutes to thirty minutes, to reduce exposure;
- include plenty of physical activity to keep the children warm, such as running and hiding games, Follow My Leader, Simon Says, etc.;
- remove any water-based activities from your planning;
- if you are concerned about the weather conditions and have doubts about running the group, trust your instincts and cancel.

Heatstroke and heat exhaustion

Heatstroke occurs when the body's temperature becomes dangerously high, and requires immediate emergency medical treatment. The precursor to heatstroke is heat exhaustion, which if not treated in time can develop into heatstroke.

Symptoms (of heat exhaustion):

- very hot skin
- flushed complexion
- excessive sweating
- very tired
- fast heartbeat
- confusion
- nausea and/or vomiting.

NB: If the condition develops into heatstroke, the person may suddenly stop sweating due to a lack of fluid available in the body. Their temperature may become dangerously high and their behaviour may become erratic and confused.

Treatment:

- call an ambulance immediately if you have any concerns;
- while waiting, move the child to a sheltered, cool area;
- ensure that another adult is with the child at all times to support them and monitor their condition;
- if they are still conscious, help the child drink sips of water;
- strip them down to let their skin cool;
- lay wet cloths across their skin and fan them.

How to avoid it in the first place:

- if the weather is very hot, remove running-based or physical games and activities from your planning;
- add water-based games and activities (see activity bank in Chapter 8 for ideas);
- only allow children who are appropriately dressed to participate;
- use the shaded areas of your site for all activities;
- if possible, put up extra shelter, such as a tarp strung between four uprights or sun tents, to keep the direct sunlight off the children;
- schedule your group to finish before 11am or start after 2pm to avoid the hottest part of the day;
- provide plenty of extra water for drinking;
- if you do not think your site is sheltered enough and you have concerns about the children's potential exposure to the heat of the sun, cancel the session.

Providing shelter

In all weathers, you will be grateful of some shelter. Your site may have plenty of tree cover in the summer, but this will thin out considerably as the trees lose their leaves. Provide something in addition, such as an awning, some sun tents, a gazebo, or a tarp strung up between four uprights. Bear in mind that if you do not have access to an indoor area on your site you will also need a sheltered, dry area for people to leave their belongings during the session.

If you are using a tarp, buy a large sized one, at least three metres by four metres, and make sure that it has reinforced holes in the corners. Get some long lengths of rope which you can thread through the holes, and simply tie each corner to an upright – such as a tree or a fence post – and tighten to stretch the tarp out. If it rains you will find that the water collects in the middle, forming a growing bulge! You can untie two of the ropes and then retie them lower down to help the water trickle down to the ground. These instructions are intentionally simple, but for niftier ways to rig up a tarp shelter just look online.

Adult-to-child ratios

The ratio of adults to children helps you to work out how many adults you will need with your group, based on the number of children attending. These ratios are calculated by the government and used by childcare settings.

Due to the young ages that we are working with, the adult-to-child ratio is quite high; one adult to every three children for those under two years, and one adult to every four children between two to three years of age.

If you are running a parent-and-child group where the parent or carer stays for the duration of the session, you will be covered, although it is good practice to have another adult working with you to help with setting up, running activities and assisting in an emergency. If you are working from an existing childcare setting, you will need to follow the regulations governing provision at your type of setting.

If you are running an independent group where the parents drop off their children and then collect them at the end of the session, you will need to ensure that you not only have the correct ratio of adults to children, but that those adults also have appropriate childcare qualifications and have been given a clear DBS check, as explained in Chapter 4. Further details of these requirements can be found online at the Department of Education website, under Early Years provision.

Site boundaries

Most of you will have chosen a site which has clear boundaries, because it will be linked to toilet facilities. You will therefore have fences or hedges containing the site on most sides, and it will be easy to keep tabs on who is coming in or leaving – both child and adult.

If you have chosen a site which has no boundaries at all, for example a patch of woodland, you are exposing your group to several risks.

- Getting lost: it will be easy for a child to stray outside of the area the rest of your group are playing in, and disappear from view.
- Problems for the search party: if there are no boundaries around the site, it is impossible to know which direction the search party should head in to find the missing child.
- Access to strangers and dogs: members of the general public and their dogs, running around off their leads, can approach the edges of your activity area or even come right into it.

As stated in Chapter 3, I would advise you not to choose an area like this at all. If you have done so, I would expect you to be running a parent-and-child group where each child has one-to-one supervision for the whole session, but that still would not fully mitigate the risks outlined above.

Risk assessment

A suggested template for your risk assessment is given in the Appendices of this book. Broadly speaking, you will need to consider the following:

- access to and from the site (if leaving your childcare setting, or if children are having to walk from a car park some way from the site);
- moving around the site safely;
- canopy level, e.g. low-hanging branches, dead branches waiting to fall;
- scrub level, e.g. thorny bushes, tree stumps;
- ground level, e.g. tree roots, slippery patches, uneven ground, protruding rocks;
- generic activities such as gathering materials, making holes in the soil, hiding and finding things, maintaining hygiene, e.g. washing hands after each session, no eating or putting things in mouths during the session;
- first aid provision for simple injuries such as cuts and stings, and a named first aider and procedure if something more serious happens, e.g. concussion;
- names of children in your group who have epipens or inhalers to manage a condition (if setting up your own group, you would ask this when parents are registering their child and request that they always bring the relevant medication with them).

If you find the idea of doing this daunting, use a copy of the risk assessment template in this book, adding your own thoughts to it as you go. But don't ignore the need to do one! While no amount of paperwork can prevent the accident that was unforeseen, you have a moral obligation to "prevent the preventable" by noting and removing risks around the site and your planned activities.

How many risk assessments do I need?

This depends on whether you are operating as part of an existing childcare setting – in which case you will be subject to their rules and regulations – or running your own group.

If you are setting up your own group, you will need to discuss risk assessment with the site representative, but as a minimum you should complete an assessment like the one given in the Appendices.

This will ensure that you have assessed the site itself for risks, and also included generic activities which you will carry out on a regular basis, such as playing hide-and-seek or gathering and using natural materials. You and the site representative should both have a signed copy of your final risk assessment, and any changes that you make, by adding new activities, should be included in a regular update for the site representative. The frequency of this update will depend on how often you change your risk assessment – if you regularly add new activities, once a month might be a good idea.

When you are coming up with new ideas for activities, make sure that you bear the following in mind:

- Are the resources for this activity safe for children to use?
- Has the proposed activity area been checked for safety concerns?
- Will the children be able to follow the activity?
- Is the ratio of adults to children available for this activity adequate?

Accidents and emergencies

Completing a risk assessment, planning activities carefully and checking your site, resources and equipment will go a long way to prevent any accidents. However, you will need a trained first aider at every session along with a first aid kit and fully charged mobile phone in case the unexpected happens.

First aid training

According to current guidance, at least one of the people leading or working with your outdoor group will need to be trained in first aid. Don't cross your fingers and hope that one of the parents in attendance will know what to do – it's your job as group leader to take charge in the event of an accident or medical emergency.

Various providers offer Ofsted-approved, paediatric, first aid courses which deal specifically with infants and young children. Find one in your local area and attend; if you are making a funding bid to set up your group, include the cost of your training in the total. As mentioned earlier, if you have chosen a remote site you will need to have paediatric outdoor first aid training from an accredited provider.

First aid kit

If you work within an existing childcare setting, you will already have access to first aid resources. If not, purchase one of the "small standard workplace compliant" first aid kits available from St Johns Ambulance or other safety organisations.

You might also want to bring a blanket for making a child who is unwell or injured comfortable, but you **must** bring your fully charged mobile phone to each group session.

Giving your location to the emergency services

You will need to give clear directions to the emergency services so that they can find your group. In the heat of the moment, you might be administering first aid and need someone else to do this. Write down the full postal address of the venue you are using on a piece of card, along with any other useful directions for finding the site, and tuck it inside your first aid kit. You can ask someone else to read these to the operator while you administer first aid.

If your location is a short walk from the road, you will need to send another adult to meet the ambulance and guide them to you and the casualty. Bear this in mind when choosing a site for your group, and also when calculating adult-to-child ratios if running an independent group where the parents do not stay.

Accident and evacuation procedure

We have already talked about being prepared to deal with a casualty during a session. On very rare occasion you might also need to evacuate; that is, ensure that everyone in the group leaves the site quickly and safely.

It is sensible to have a written procedure for both of these eventualities, so that you are clear in your own mind about who will do what, and so is anyone else working with you. This will help you and the other adults to stay calm and focused, which in turn will comfort the children.

In a situation requiring first aid and the emergency services, you will need to know who is going to administer first aid, who will call the ambulance and who will keep the rest of the group occupied and away from the casualty. In the event of an evacuation, you will need to identify in advance a safe place where the group will go, who will lead and do a headcount to ensure that everyone is present, and who will bring up the rear.

If you are the sole leader of a group with parents staying, it is reasonable to assume that one of them could call the emergency services per your instructions, while you administer first aid. If there is no one else to lead activities while you are looking after the casualty, your procedure will state that you will give the other parents clear instructions to move their children away from the casualty and play elsewhere. Likewise, in the event of an evacuation you will give clear instructions to the parents about where to go, and bring up the rear yourself, doing a headcount on arrival.

Other useful procedures

Ideally you will have found a private area for your site, but if members of the public can walk through it or by it, you need a **dogs and strangers procedure** on how to deal with unwanted advances made by strangers or dogs which are off the lead. At its simplest, you need to tell the parents, staff and children to stand still if they are approached by a dog with their hands by their sides, looking at their shoes to avoid eye contact with the animal. With strangers, adults need to approach them and firmly ask them to leave the activity area. For more advice and guidance, look online.

If your site is a couple of minutes' walk from the road you will need a **site access procedure** for accessing and leaving the site. This can be as simple as waiting until a specified time, in a safe area near where people park their cars, and then all walking down to the site together.

If there are going to be any other adults working with you, it would be wise to have a **behaviour management procedure** where you agree what techniques you will use to encourage co-operative play, such as turn-taking and playing gently with each other. This will ensure that you and your team have agreed how you will deal with issues that arise during the session, even if they way that has been agreed upon differs from how they discipline their own children at home.

6 Spread the word!

In this chapter we will look at:

- offline and online publicity for your group;
- communication with parents and carers;
- Information Sheets and Joining Letters;
- creating a positive relationship with parents.

Offline publicity

Most of us are so used to searching online for services and information that it's easy to forget the value of offline publicity and communication. But posters are cheap to produce, easy to read and can go wherever you're allowed to stick them! You will want to choose places where parents and children regularly congregate, and get the permission of the owner or workers before putting yours up.

Here is a quick list of possible places:

- libraries
- health centres
- toy shops
- cafes
- soft play venues
- leisure centres

- community centres
- post offices
- supermarket community boards
- Sure Start or equivalent children's centres.

The key to an effective poster is one which is easy to read from a distance and has contact information clearly displayed. Consider including the following details:

- name of group
- type of group, e.g. parent and toddler
- what day/time it runs
- a few typical activities, e.g. games, simple crafts and exploring the outdoors
- phone number or email for further information (ideally, include both).

When it comes to poster design, there is always plenty more information that you *could* include. However, most of that additional information can be included in an Information Sheet (see below).

You can also produce fliers and leave them in a pile at the kinds of places listed above. The advantage of a flier is that the interested person takes the contact information away with them. The disadvantage is that they can cost a lot more to produce.

Online

There are plenty of ways to publicise your group online, including social media sites and online forums.

Forums for parenting or local communities

Some sites such as Netmums have a noticeboard for activities in your local area, and at the time of writing it's free to add your listing. You could also try searching for an online community forum which offers free listings for local residents about clubs and activities.

Email

Providing an email address on your publicity makes it easy for interested parents to contact you and for you to send them information in return. Setting up an email address with your group's name in the title is a nice touch, e.g. littlehedgehogs@emailprovider.com, and will seem more professional than using your personal email address, especially if it contains a nickname.

Social media

Once your group is up and running, you may wish to publicise it further by updating a page on a social media site about your activities with photos and messages. This could be a very effective marketing tool to encourage other parents to try the group, as they can see pictures and comments about it.

We are used to seeing a lot more information about each other online these days, but consider your own privacy in all this. It will look more professional if you create a new account which is just for your toddler group and its associates, and better protect your privacy.

You might also bear in mind that a page which is rarely updated might not be the best advert for your group; if you don't have time to post pictures, tips or activity ideas on a regular basis (say once a week) then maybe it's better not to bother at all.

Using photos of children to promote your group

If you or other practitioners wish to photograph the children attending your group, bear in mind that some parents will not want images of their children appearing in promotional material for your business. This should be respected. There are other child protection issues around using photos of children, so you will need to follow the guidelines below.

- Obtain written permission from the parent or carer who regularly attends with the child before using their photo.
- If the parent looks uncomfortable or does not agree straight away, do not use it – they don't have to give a reason why.
- When using permitted photos, do not name the child in the photo or any accompanying caption or comment.
- Do not use any full face photos, but instead pictures where the children are engaged in activity.

Domestic violence and child abuse are issues which unfortunately affect some families, and you are never going to know which children in your group might be protected by court orders. You will also be unaware of which children are adopted or fostered, and again, their carers may be actively protecting them from contact with their biological parent(s). Following the guidelines above will give you and your other practitioners the reassurance that you are not inadvertently putting a child at risk.

By phone

If you work for an established nursery or childcare setting, you will probably put the main contact number on your publicity, and give the secretary or business manager instructions on how to deal with the call.

If you are setting this up as a self-employed business venture, or in partnership with other parents and helpers, a phone number is essential for allowing interested parents to contact you. You will need to consider whether to buy a separate pay-as-you-go mobile phone, because using your personal mobile to store the numbers, handle calls and reply to texts may leave you out of pocket and confused about who's who in your phonebook list. The disadvantage is the additional cost, lugging another mobile around and the risk of losing it.

If you're using your own mobile, a couple of useful tips are below:

- When storing names and numbers of interested callers, do so with an unusual prefix such as ZZ. This will make your phone store all the numbers for your group together, making it easy to scroll through the list and contact one or all of them.
- Text in reply to phone messages, asking for an email address to which you can send an Information Sheet (see below). You can then follow up with interested parents either online or by phone call.

Communication with parents

Good communication between you and the parents and carers will create an atmosphere of trust and friendliness.

You can help this process by providing useful, clear advice about what the group is going to be like when they are considering whether to join. This is called an Information Sheet. Once they have signed up, you can also prime them for the first few sessions by sending out a Joining Letter with any more useful information you feel appropriate. These two letters are explained below.

If you are running an outdoor session as part of your childcare setting's daily provision, you will probably include all children in it as a matter of course, and will not need to seek special permission to do so unless you are leaving the nursery to visit a different site. If so, check requirements for advising parents and carers with your nursery head and proceed accordingly.

Information Sheet

The purpose of this document is to give enough information about the group for the interested parent or carer to decide whether to attend. With this in mind, consider including the following:

- where your group will be held;
- how long each session will last;
- the age range for children attending;
- who runs it (this could be a childcare setting, existing group or individual);
- typical activities (provide at least five);
- facilities available onsite, e.g. toilets, hand-washing facilities. If people will be changing nappies under the trees and cleaning their hands with wet wipes and sterilisation gel, they need some warning!;
- how to book a place;
- who to call with a query.

If you are charging for the session:

- how much the sessions cost;
- how to pay;
- your policy on bringing along an additional child within the age range (often, the second child gets a discounted rate);
- your policy on bringing along babies under 1 (it will be best to admit them free of charge as they will sleep through most of it!);
- your cancellation or refund policy (this need only be a sentence explaining under what circumstances you offer a refund, e.g. if the group does not run one week because the leader is unable to attend).

The information provided should fit on one side of A4 in font size 12, and can be emailed or posted to the interested party.

Joining Letter

When a booking or payment has been received, send the Joining Letter. This will contain the information they need to find the site, clarify rules about safety and hygiene, and reiterate your cancellation policy. Sending it will ensure that you have fulfilled your part in setting their expectations and putting any important details in writing. Once again, this needs to fit on an A4 sheet of paper and can be emailed or posted. Consider including the following in your Joining Letter:

- Full address of site: include postcode for people using satnav, and suggestions for nearby parking if none is available outside.
- What to wear: you might think that this is unnecessary, but it's astonishing how many people will roll up in a hoody and trainers on a rainy day. There is no harm

reminding people to wrap up warm, bring wellies and wear waterproof coats! Also, remind them that on sunny hot days they will need to bring sunblock, sunhats and extra water for their children to drink.

- Hygiene: remind parents about facilities available onsite for toileting and hand washing. It is good practice to provide wet wipes and anti-bacterial gel for children and parents to use, even if facilities are available on site.

- Food and drink: assuming that you will not be providing any during your session, it is up to parents to bring their own supplies. However, you should clearly state that children should not eat or drink during the session without cleaning their hands first (this is particularly important on farm land or land grazed by animals).

- Safety: if you are running a group where parents stay, state clearly that it is the parent's responsibility to keep the child safe at all times and to supervise them during activities.

- Cancellation and refund policy: clarify whether a refund is given to parents who pay in advance but don't turn up (it is acceptable not to offer a refund if you have made it clear that this will be the case). You will also want to remind parents that the group takes place whatever the weather, and that in the event that you need to cancel, you will text/email them all at least one hour beforehand. Whether you offer a refund for the session which you could not deliver is your decision, but it would be good customer service to do so.

Working with parents: a positive relationship

Knowing that parents or carers will also attend your group can be quite nerve-wracking. Why? Because parents will expect a professional, well-organised service – even more so if they are paying for it. They will expect you to be on time, organised, competent and unflappable. Considering that you are working with their children, this is entirely reasonable.

They may also have some misgivings about doing a group outside – what about the weather? Will my child like it? – and will want to be able to trust your judgement in the activities planned. To smooth the path to good relations, present yourself and your group professionally. In particular, bear the following points in mind:

- Keep accurate records of phone numbers, addresses and so on, because people will not want to give them again and again.

- Check any communications that you send, be they emails, fliers, texts or letters, for spelling mistakes or other typos.

- Provide receipts promptly for any payments.

- Ensure that your site and activities are fully prepared before the children arrive.

- Start and end the session on time.
- Always pack enough resources for all the children to have a go.
- Be available for parents to chat to before and after the session.

Make the division of responsibilities clear

Children are used to their parents being the main authority in their lives, and will find it confusing if you to take on this responsibility during the session. Be clear with parents and carers: your responsibility is to plan suitable activities and provide adequate and appropriate resources. Theirs is to keep their child safe and under control during the session.

Be confident in your plans

Outdoor learning and Forest Schools are very current ideas and everyone will have suggestions based on what they've heard about elsewhere, such as having fires for cooking or using hand tools.

By all means, bear the well-meaning comments of others in mind, but don't feel obliged to change your planned activities to accommodate their whims. You and your practitioners have sweated over the detail of activities you deem appropriate for this age range and site, and are better placed to decide on what to do than the parents are (whatever their views on this!) Changing plans on the hoof will be confusing for everyone; carry out your plans and reflect upon the outcomes afterwards, noting what worked well and what would need tweaking next time to make it more successful. For more guidance on planning, see Chapter 7.

Listen to gripes and grumbles

Bear in mind two things about complaining: firstly, if people are paying for a service they feel entitled to make demands, and secondly, some people are never happy!

If you are approachable and answer people's questions in a friendly and helpful way, this will set most misunderstandings straight before they become a problem. If you're running well-organised and resourced sessions that most parents seem perfectly happy with, you can use that to balance out any grumbles that come your way.

Listen politely to what they say, though; you may discover that it's because they are anxious or unsure about the outdoor group format and need a bit more reassurance about the purpose of the activities.

7 | Planning

In this chapter we will look at:

- different group types and their planning requirements;
- different planning formats to suit your group, and how to use the planning templates included with this book;
- reflecting on outcomes to get the most from your planning;
- health and safety – why we include it.

Different group types

Below are some different group types which might work for your setup.

Childcare setting group

By this, I mean an outdoor toddler group led by professional childcare practitioners, such as childminders or nursery workers. There would be no parents in attendance and it is likely that the group would run for forty-five minutes to one hour as part of that nursery/childminder group's scheduled activity for the day. This type of session might have a theme and the children would all participate in a series of activities over the course of the session.

Childcare setting carousel

This type of group is similar to above, with a key difference that various activities are taking place in parallel, each led by a different childcare practitioner. The children would be able to move around the different activities and try them out during the allotted time. The group might start and end with everyone together singing songs, sharing a story or in some other communal activity.

Drop-in carousel

This type of group is one where parents accompany their children and can arrive whenever they want during an allotted time period, participating in some or all of the activities available. This type of group tends to run for an hour and a half to two hours to maximise the number of people attending. Each member of staff will have an activity which they run on repeat during the session, as parents and children wander around choosing what to do next.

Parent and toddler group

This type of group has a fixed start and end time for all children and parents attending, and tends to start and end with everyone together for songs, stories and so on. The middle part of the session might have different activities running in parallel, or all children following a series of activities if there is only one practitioner. Parents are expected to help their children with activities throughout the session.

Independently run, no parents

Parents or carers will drop their child off at an agreed time and then collect them perhaps an hour later. This gives you less flexibility to shorten the sessions if the weather is a concern (see Chapter 5) and puts you *in loco parentis*, ensuring the welfare of each child in the absence of the parent. As described earlier in this book, this type of group is the most complicated to set up and run because you will be responsible for ensuring that all adults working with you hold appropriate childcare qualifications to work with this age range, as well as clean Disclosure and Barring Service checks. You will also need to find out how to register them as your employees if you are paying them, follow any relevant employer legislation and hold insurance to cover all staff.

How to plan

Some of you might be wondering if this is necessary. After all, isn't the whole point of outdoor learning and play the creative, spontaneous stuff? I agree that those experiences are memorable for adults and children alike, but they are far less likely to arise if your sessions are pure chaos from start to end. Planning what you will do helps to:

- ensure that all resources are brought to the site;
- provide enough for all children to participate;
- designate different areas of the site to different activities;
- agree roles and responsibilities with other staff members;
- consider risk and ensure activities are suitable;
- know what to do with early finishers.

This will give all the adults working with you confidence to get on with their tasks and devote their attention to the children, rather than wondering what is happening next. It will also allow you to set up the activities quickly and easily, and make you (if you are leading things) feel more relaxed as the session starts. The parents attending will also relax if they can see things running smoothly.

Which planning template will suit my group best?

The following templates are in the Appendices of this book:

- Planning template 1: this can be used for planning a series of activities that all the children participate in, i.e. childcare setting, parent and toddler group with one leader.
- Planning template 2: this can be used for planning a carousel of activities with a shared start and end to the session, i.e. parent and toddler group with more practitioners, childcare setting.
- Planning template 3: this can be used for planning a drop-in carousel with no shared beginning or end activities.

Feel free to adapt these templates as you see fit. The idea is to provide an outline for planning your sessions so that you can write down the activities, preparation and resources required for them. You may find that over time you want to increase or decrease the activities offered, or the order of activities. The Planning Templates can be found in the Appendices section at the back of this book.

How long should the session be?

Forty-five minutes to an hour is a good amount of time to be outside when you're very young. This will also sound like a reasonable timeslot to parents if you're charging a small fee for their children to attend. If you're running a group within an existing child-care setting, you will have your own policies and guidance to follow.

You will find that the children get through a *lot* of different activities in one hour and can start to get tired, meaning that they are less interested in joining in and more likely to start fussing. The weather will also make a difference to what they can put up with. I am a staunch advocate of playing outside whatever the weather and would only cancel a group in the teeth of a hurricane, but very cold weather is hard on the littlest children because their hands and feet can become painfully cold. They are also the least mobile, so they can't get warm by playing running games. If the weather is bitterly cold, you can agree with the parents or other staff to shorten the session to thirty minutes and make sure that the children stay as active as possible. If some of the children turn up in clothing which is not going to keep them warm and dry enough, either loan them some spares or politely but firmly advise the parent that they will not be able to participate today.

Drop-ins are slightly different. If you are running a drop-in you will need to make it one and a half to two hours long so that the maximum number of people can come. You will need to wrap yourself up pretty warm too if you're going to be outside for that long!

How can I provide activities suitable for one year olds and three year olds at the same time?

The difference in mobility, communication and comprehension between a one year old and a three year old is enormous. This can make planning activities seem daunting; how on earth can you find something which will suit a busy, bustling three year old and a placid, gurgling one year old?

The secret is to start and end each session together, so that the children get the pleasure of participating in songs and stories as a group, but plan a carousel of activities in between, some of which are suited to each end of your spectrum. For the very youngest in your group, you will need something like treasure baskets, baby obstacle courses and a protected area for them to explore by crawling and cruising.

For the older children who can run, climb and talk, you will want a range of games, crafts and building activities. See the activity bank in Chapter 8 for more ideas.

Planning by activity

This is simply choosing a range of interesting and fun sounding activities to fill your session. Try and pick a range of types, such as craft, games, songs and physical activities.

Planning by theme

This works by choosing activities which are all linked by a theme for the session, for example: telling a story about a hedgehog who had lost his way home, then making a nest for the hedgehog, learning a song with some actions about the hedgehog, and playing a game where the children curl up into a ball, just like hedgehogs do. You can use national holidays as a theme (such as Easter, Christmas or Bonfire Night) or storybooks. Examples of thematic planning using books are given after the Activity Bank in Chapter 8.

Reflecting on outcomes to improve planning

To get the full benefit of planning your sessions, you should reflect on how it all went afterwards. This is to capitalise on the things that went well, and to find solutions for the hiccups so that they don't come back next time.

Try to spend fifteen minutes going over the following questions. If you are working with other staff, include them in this process to get their views too. You can do this as soon as you've cleared up, or later on the same day, jotting your thoughts on your copy of the plan. You can include any aspects of your group here: the activities, positive or negative comments made by the children or parents, the weather, the site or facilities.

- What went well today, and why?
- What caused problems, and why?
- What can we do to avoid those problems next time?
- Any other ideas for next session?

Health and safety

You might have noticed that each planning template has a note about "health and safety" on it. This is a prompt to include useful information for parents and children about what to be aware of during the session. This is a useful thing to include because as soon as you've told the children's parents to watch out for the nettle bed in the corner, it's their responsibility to keep their child out of it, not yours!

A health and safety announcement need only take a minute or two at the beginning of the session. The kind of things I would include in my health and safety announcement at the beginning of any session would be:

- mentioning where nettles and brambles are;
- advise them of where any really uneven ground is;
- telling them how to find the toilets;
- letting them know where the wet wipes and antibacterial gel are kept if their child's hands get very dirty;
- telling them who the trained first aider is for today;
- pointing out any area which is off-limits for the session and explaining why;
- asking them if they have any questions.

If you do this every week, you might feel like you're repeating yourself, but you're also helping out any new people who have just joined . . . And also reminding those who came last week but weren't listening too closely.

8 | Activity bank

In this chapter we will look at:

- a range of possible activities for your group;
- planning activities for one year olds;
- using storybooks;
- a brief introduction to thematic planning.

Most of this chapter is an activity bank, full of ideas for you to use when planning your sessions. Over sixty activity ideas are included, grouped by activity type. Each activity indicates the age range that it is suitable for, what you will need and how to prepare and lead it. It also indicates whether the activity is dependent on the season. The ones marked "all year round" are all suitable for use all the time, but especially handy in the depths of Winter when the trees are bare!

If you are new to planning, the idea is that you take the planning template from the Appendices which best suits your group and then choose a range of activities to fill the boxes on the plan. Try to pick a mix of activity types for each session.

The rest of this chapter looks at how to accommodate the youngest children in your plans, and using storybooks as a starting point for thematic planning. If you are completely new to planning activities for children, you might find it easier to start with simply choosing activities as described above, and then move on to thematic planning when you have built up some experience.

I hope that the ideas in this section will get you started with your group. But more than that, I hope that they inspire you to come up with some more ideas, much better than these ones. When it comes to planning activities for your group, the sky's the limit – as long as you've got the resources, you've planned out how to do it and you know it's appropriate for the age of the children, you can let your imagination run wild.

Games and physical activities

Hanging Hoops

Activity type: Game/physical

Age range: 2–3 years

Season: All year round

Resources: 4–6 plastic hoops, lengths of rope

Preparation:
Tie each hoop securely to one end of a rope, and then tie the rope from a tree branch or overhead beam so that the hoop is suspended just above the ground. You want the children to be able to crawl or climb through the hoops, so make sure they are no more than 30cm above the ground. Create a trail around your site for the children to climb and crawl through.

Procedure:
Lead the children around, showing them the hoops and how to climb or crawl through them.

Ask parents to guide their children through the activity or assign an adult to help if parents are not present.

Practitioner's note:
If you want to incorporate a story with this activity, where the children follow you around as you tell it, it will work really well. A good one is *We're Going on a Bear Hunt* by Michael Rosen.

Obstacle Adventure

Activity type: Game/physical

Age range: 2–3 years

Season: All year round

Resources: Hoops, ropes, planks, crates, buckets, bean bags, anything else you can think of!

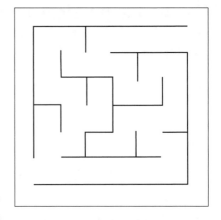

Preparation:
Set up an "obstacle course" for the children to complete, such as: ropes laid in a spiral on the ground that the children have to run around; logs for balancing on; a crate to climb over; a play tunnel to crawl through; hanging hoops; bean bags to collect and throw into a bucket.

Procedure:
Show the children the course, and model how to do each bit.

Encourage the children to try the bits they think look interesting (don't expect them to complete this in order, or in its entirety).

Practitioner's note:
If it's hot, include a "water feature" such as a paddling pool that they have to jump across.

Ensure all equipment used is safe and sturdy.

Find the Treasure!

Activity type: Game/physical

Age range: 1–3 years

Season: All year round

Resources: "Treasure chest" or some other special container, such as a shoebox covered in shiny paper and stickers; 10–20 pieces of "treasure", such as bean bags, plastic balls; other objects related to a story.

Preparation:
Hide the treasure objects around your site. Choose items that are easy to spot due to their bright colour.

Procedure:
If you are using a story to launch this activity, sit the children in a circle and tell them a story about some treasure that goes missing.

Next ask the children to help find the hidden objects. Explain that they need to search around the whole site. Tell them what they are looking for – you might want to hold one of the objects up so that they can see what you mean.

When they find one they bring it back and put it in the treasure chest.
At the end of the game, invite the children to help you count how many items you have collected.

Practitioner's note:
You can repeat this game by splitting the group in half. One half hides the objects and the others then go and find them, and vice versa.

Bags in the Pot

Activity type: Game/physical

Age range: 2–3 years

Season: All year round

Resources: Bean bags or medium sized pine cones, buckets, hoops.

Preparation:
Set up a row of buckets.

Procedure:
Children try to throw the bean bags into the bucket from where they're standing.

   Once they have all gone in, they can tip them out and start again or leave it for the next children to play.

Practitioner's note:
If you don't have bean bags you could also use the type of small plastic ball that you find in ball pits for this activity, or modify it to use small sticks and twigs.

Hungry Bears

Activity type: Game/physical

Age range: 2–3 years old

Season: All year round

Resources: Toy food or real food such as pota-
toes or carrots, five large hoops (different col-
ours if possible).

Preparation:
Lay the hoops out on the ground in the shape
of the dots on the five side of a dice (four corners and one in the middle).
   Put all the pieces of food in the middle hoop.

Procedure:
Ask the parents/adults to wait by one of the corner hoops with their child. Make sure
that there are some parents and children standing at each of the corner hoops before the
game starts.
   Explain that they are hungry bears waking up after hibernating, and they need to find
some food. Explain that when you call out their coloured hoop, e.g. "yellow bears, time
for lunch!" they need to run and collect as much food as they can from the centre hoop,
putting it into their team hoop.
   When you want to swap groups, get the current team to stop by calling out, "yellow
bears, time to go to sleep!" and they have to return to their hoop and lie down.
   Call out one coloured hoop at a time. Once all the food has gone from the centre
hoop, it is fine for the children to collect food from the other bears' hoops.

Practitioner's note:
You will definitely need adults to play this game, as the children will not fully understand
the rules otherwise! Be patient and play it regularly, and they will learn them.

What's the Time, Mr. Wolf?

Activity type: Game/physical

Age range: 1–3 years (see Practitioner's Note below)

Season: All year round

Resources: Nothing

Preparation: None

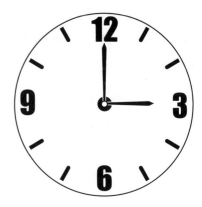

Procedure:
One adult is the wolf. They walk around the site, with the children walking a few paces behind them.

Every time the wolf has walked a few more steps, the children call out, "what's the time, Mr. Wolf?" The wolf turns round and shouts out a time in reply, e.g. "3 o'clock", and then carries on walking.

If the wolf shouts, "dinner time!" then all the children have to run away as fast as they can. The wolf, meanwhile, runs after the children and tries to catch one.

The child who is caught can either be the wolf next time round (this works well if the parent is with them) or they can stand with the wolf for the next round of the game and help the wolf to catch someone else for his dinner.

Practitioner's note:
Children who are not very mobile can play this game if they are carried by a grown-up.

Catch a Mouse

Activity type: Game/physical

Age range: 2–3 years

Season: All year round

Resources: Nothing

Preparation: None

Procedure:
An adult is the mouse and stands with her back to the rest of the group – the cats – who are lined up some distance away, e.g. at least ten metres.

The game starts when the children call, "Little mouse, can you see me?" and the mouse replies, "not yet!" The cats then creep up to the mouse while her back is turned. The object of the game is to touch the mouse before she sees that you are there. The mouse, meanwhile, is allowed to turn round whenever she wants.

Every time the mouse turns around, the children have to stop moving and stay as still as possible. If the mouse sees them moving, she can call their name out and ask them to go back to the starting line. The winner is the first person to reach the mouse while her back is turned. The winner can then be the mouse if they want.

Practitioner's note:
Little children will not be able to stand very still, so focus instead on whether they are still running or have tried to stop.

The children will need help from adults to learn the rules to this game.

Follow the Leader

Activity type: Game/physical

Age range: 1–3 years (see Practitioner's Note)

Season: All year round

Resources: None

Preparation:
If you want to incorporate something like climbing through a hoop or walking along a rope trail, lay this out before the game starts.

Procedure:
One adult is the leader. Start off standing in a circle facing each other. The leader chooses which movement to make. The object of the game is for the others to copy the leader's actions.

You can walk around the site as you play this game, so that ways of moving – jumping, running, crawling or rolling – can also be incorporated.

If you see that some of the group are waylaid, stop walking around and do some Follow the Leader actions standing in one place so they can catch you up.

Practitioner's note:
If you are playing this with very young children, sit in a circle and use arm, hand and head movements. Keep making the movement, such as touching your nose or patting your knees with your hands, while they are working out how to copy you.

Simon Says

Activity type: Game/physical

Age range: 2–3 years

Season: All year round

Resources: None

Preparation: None

Procedure:
Sit or stand in a circle.

One person is Simon, and they call out different actions for the children to copy.

If you want to make it a bit harder, try telling the children to only copy you if you say, "Simon says" before each command.

Once the game is established you can let volunteer children lead the game by demonstrating an action that they want their peers to copy.

Practitioner's note:
Hopping is quite tricky for this age range – try jumping instead.

Don't be too fastidious about whether the children noticed you saying "Simon says" or not – they will be happy just to watch and join in.

Train Trails

Activity type: Game/physical

Age range: 1–3 years (see Practitioner's Note)

Season: All year round

Resources: Chalk, ropes.

Preparation:
If using rope, lay the ropes across your site. The idea
is that they will be train tracks, so lay them in inter-
esting shapes, like spirals and twirls as well as straight. If you have a large site, you could
lay them as tracks leading to each activity.

   If using chalk (see Practitioner's Note) mark the tracks on the ground.

Procedure:
Explain to the children that you're all getting on a pretend train today and travelling to
each of the activities.

   Ask the children for noises that a train makes, and practice making them together.

   Line up, with an adult at the front to call out, "all aboard!" and then start moving
along the tracks.

   The rest of the group follows the track behind the leader, making train noises and trying to keep their feet on the rope trail.

   As the children learn how to play this game, you can add other calls and commands
to their repertoire, e.g. "going through a tunnel!" or "stopping at the station!" and agree
which noises or actions they need to make.

Practitioner's note:
Make sure that you clear the ropes up after this game so that no child can play with them
unsupervised.

Hide and Seek

Activity type: Game/physical

Age range: 1–3 years (see Practitioner's Note)

Season: Late Spring to late Autumn

Resources: Things to hide behind or in – trees, bushes, tents, tunnels, giant cardboard boxes, etc.

Preparation:
If your site does not have much by way of natural hiding places, lay out some objects like those listed above which could be used.

Procedure:
One person goes to hide, while the rest sit in a circle with their hands over their eyes. Count to twenty out loud, and then call, "coming ready or not!"

Find the person hiding and all return to the circle. The finder can be the next person to hide.

Practitioner's note:
It's common for children to think that they are hiding if they cannot see anyone else, e.g. sitting in plain sight with their hands over their eyes. To ensure that they do actually hide, play with adults or parents assisting.

Never play hide and seek in a setting where the child could be out of sight for a couple of minutes, on a site with no clear boundaries or where the general public can gain access.

Sleepy Sheep

Activity type: Game/physical

Age range: 2–3 years (see Practitioner's Note)

Season: All year round

Resources: Things to hide behind or in – trees, bushes, tents, tunnels, giant cardboard boxes, etc.

Preparation:

If your site does not have much by way of natural hiding places, lay out some objects like those listed above which could be used.

Procedure:

An adult is the shepherd, and leads the rest of the group – the sheep – around the site.

When the shepherd announces, "time for bed, little sheep!" the rest of the group has to curl up on the ground and close their eyes.

The shepherd taps one of the sheep on the head, and they then run off to hide.

When the shepherd says, "time to wake up, little sheep!" the rest of the group open their eyes and try to work out who is missing before going to look for them.

Practitioner's note:

You will need adults to help the children to follow the rules for this game. Don't be too much of a stickler for getting them exactly right – there is a lot here for little ones to remember.

It's common for children to think that they are hiding if they cannot see anyone else, e.g. sitting in plain sight with their hands over their eyes. To ensure that they do actually hide, play with adults or parents assisting.

The Name Game

Activity type: Game/physical

Age range: 2–3 years

Season: All year round

Resources: None

Preparation: None

> John, Martin, Mary, Sanjay, Lucy, Sarah,

Procedure:
Sit in a circle. One person starts by saying the name of someone else in the circle, e.g. Josh, and they both swap places. Once they have sat down in their new places, Josh calls out a name of someone else, e.g. Ava, and they swap places and sit down. Now Ava calls out a name of someone, and they swap. Make sure that no one is missed out. This game is a good way to learn names quickly.

Practitioner's note:
Some children will need help in remembering the others' names, so being paired with an adult will help here.

Younger children will not be able to remember the names of others or maybe have difficulty saying them, so the leader can call out a pair who need to swap places, e.g. "Ava swap with Josh".

Fruit Salad

Activity type: Game/physical

Age range: 1–3 years (see Practitioner's Note)

Season: All year round

Resources: None

Preparation: None

Procedure:
Sit in a circle. Go round and label each child as a
fruit – use four, such as orange, apple, strawberry, grape.

   Call out a fruit, e.g. grape, and the children who are "grapes" have to stand and swap places with someone else who is too. They then sit down in their new space. Call out the other fruits one at a time, mixing the order and speeding things up to make it more exciting. Ensure that no fruits are missed out.

Practitioner's note:
This game does not have to be about fruit but can be adapted to anything you want: flowers, animals, types of weather.

   It is best played with adults so that the younger children – who may not be aware of their fruit – can participate.

The Touching Game

Activity type: Game/physical

Age range: 1–3 years

Season: All year round

Resources: None, unless you want to hide something special for them to find.

Preparation: See above

Procedure:
Children sit in a circle.

The leader thinks of different things for them to find and touch, such as: a daisy, a tall tree, someone wearing a coat, a pink bag.

Once the children have touched the item the leader called out, they can come back to the circle and wait for the next one.

Practitioner's note:
Start off simple, with items close to the circle, and as the children begin to understand the game choose items which are further away for them to find.

Can You Find . . .?

Activity type: Game/physical

Age range: 1–3 years (see Practitioner's Note)

Season: All year round

Resources: None

Preparation: None

Procedure:
Sit the children in a circle. This game is a variation on the Touching Game, in that the children have to find the thing you're talking about but then bring it back with them.

Use this game to help the children explore the site, calling out things like: a shiny green leaf, a small flower, an interesting stone, something pretty.

They will need time to look around for an example and bring it back.

Briefly, go round the circle so that the children can hold up and show what they found.

Practitioner's note:
Younger children and less mobile children will need support to play this game from adults.

Hide and Seek with a Toy

Activity type: Game/physical

Age range: 1–3 years

Season: All year round

Resources: None, unless using dolls/toys

Preparation:
If using a doll/toy, hide it before the game starts.

Procedure:
Sit in a circle. If playing the game with a toy, explain that Bill the Badger (or whatever you are using) has gone missing – can anyone find him?
Encourage the children to look all around the site, and when they find him, bring him back to the circle.

　　Ask if the child who found the toy would like to hide it next. Make sure an adult helps them to hide it, while the rest of the group sits in a circle with their eyes covered. Count up to twenty out loud, and on twenty start looking.

Fly Around the Field

Activity type: Game/physical

Age range: 1–3 years

Season: All year round

Resources: None

Preparation: None

Procedure:
Stand in a circle, with children next to their parent.

The leader will choose something about the clothes the children are wearing, for example, if they've got wellies on, and call out: "If you've got wellies on, fly around the field!"

Parents pick up their child and run around the site with them before returning to the circle. The leader calls out something else, e.g. "If you're wearing red, fly around the field!" and those children wearing something red are picked up by their parents who pick up their child and run around again before returning to the circle.

Practitioner's note:
This game relies on each child having their own grown-up to "fly" them.

With older children aged three, you can play a variation called "Run Around the Field" which does not require adult assistance.

Craft and creative activities

Rocking robins

Activity type: Craft/creative

Age range: 2–3 years

Season: All year round, but particularly good for Winter

Resources: Paper plates – enough for one per child; red and brown crayons; narrow triangles cut from yellow card (for the beak); stick-on eyes or black pens to draw one on; glue sticks.

Preparation:
Fold each of the paper plates in half. Cut enough yellow triangles for one per plate – these will be the beaks.

Set out the crayons or pens that you will use.

If possible, make one of the robins in advance, so that you can show the children and other adults what they will look like when they are finished.

Procedure:
Colour in one side of the plate brown from the fold downwards, making sure to colour in a red semi-circle for the red breast.

Draw on/stick on an eye.

Use the glue stick to stick a yellow triangle on as a beak.

Set the robin down on the ground, and tap the tail end to make it rock backwards and forwards in a pecking motion.

Practitioner's note:
This simple design can be adapted for any other kind of bird – add tail feathers or crests to make more exotic ones.

Forest Crowns

Activity type: Craft/creative

Age range: 1–3 years

Season: Late Spring to Autumn

Resources: Strips of card roughly 5cm wide, any colour, long enough to fasten around a child's head; glue sticks; sellotape for fastening the crowns; leaves, flowers, grasses, etc.; buckets or collecting trays for collecting interesting things to stick on the crowns.

Preparation:
Cut the lengths of card as described above, ensuring that you have one per child.
   Set out the glue sticks and sellotape for later use.

Procedure:
Show the children and other adults how to make a forest crown.
   First collect some interesting flowers, leaves, etc. and stick on to the band of card.
   Leave a gap at one end of 5cm, so that you can fasten both ends together with the sellotape.
   To get the best fit for a child's head, wrap it round their head before fastening the ends together.

Practitioner's note:
If you want to do this activity in the Winter, provide craft materials such as scraps of coloured paper, fabrics, feathers and foil to stick on the crowns in place of the natural materials listed above.

Make an Autumn Sunshine

Activity type: Craft/creative

Age range: 1–3 years

Season: Autumn

Resources: Paper plates – one per child; glue sticks; plenty of autumn leaves, especially yellow and orange ones; strips of yellow paper or card, about 15cms long – cut enough for at least six per sunshine (these will be the sun's rays); Bluetack

Preparation:
Cut the strips of paper for the sun's rays and set out the glue sticks ready for use.

Make a sunshine in advance so that you can show the others what they look like when finished.

Procedure:
Demonstrate how to make an Autumn sunshine by collecting lots of yellow leaves, and then sticking them carefully to your plate.

Add strips of yellow card or paper around the edge of the plate to look like the sun's rays by fastening them to the rim on the back of the paper plate.

When finished, Bluetack the suns to walls/tree trunks/fences around the site.

Practitioner's note:
Children can take their suns home at the end of the session.

Leaf Prints

Activity type: Craft/creative

Age range: 1–3 years

Season: All year round (see Practitioner's Note below)

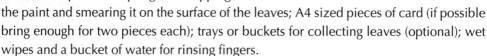

Resources: Leaves (you do not need to collect these first); ready-mixed paint in different colours; shallow dishes for paint (one colour per dish); small pieces of sponge, for dipping into the paint and smearing it on the surface of the leaves; A4 sized pieces of card (if possible bring enough for two pieces each); trays or buckets for collecting leaves (optional); wet wipes and a bucket of water for rinsing fingers.

Preparation:
Set out the paints, sponge pieces, card and cleaning materials.

Procedure:
Show the children how to pick leaves by the stalk, so that they get the whole leaf to use for printing.

Ask the children to find two really interesting leaves from around the site, to pick them and bring them back.

When the children have returned, demonstrate how to dab the sponge into the paint and then coat the surface of the leaf with it. Show how to press the leaf down on the paper, hold for a count of three and then carefully lift to leave a print.

Encourage the children to experiment with different colours of paint and different types of leaf – they can collect as many more as they want.

Practitioner's note:
If you want to make this a more communal activity, replace the individual pieces of card with an old roll of wallpaper. Unroll it so the plain back is facing upwards, and create a shared printing surface several metres long. The children can kneel alongside it and add their prints.

Although you can do this all year round, the widest variety of leaf shapes will be available from late Spring to late Autumn. If you want to do this during the Winter, try evergreens, hedges or shrubs.

Leaf Kebabs

Activity type: Craft/creative

Age range: 1–3 years

Season: Spring to the end of Autumn

Resources: Sticks – one per child; plenty of leaves of different colours and shapes

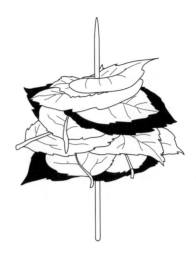

Preparation: None

Procedure:
Show the children how to make a leaf kebab by find-ing some interesting coloured or shaped leaves.

One leaf at a time, make a hole in the leaf with the tip of the stick and then push it down so that it is about two thirds down the stick.

Collect other interesting shaped and coloured leaves, and repeat until you have a thick wodge of leaves on your stick.

Practitioner's note:
You can make leaf pompoms like this too, but use a plastic darning needle and thread instead of a stick. Obviously, if you do this activity you will need to ensure that each child is working with an adult so that they won't hurt themselves on the plastic darning needle.

Mud Paintings

Activity type: Craft/creative

Age range: 1–3 years

Season: All year round

Resources: Soil – this can be dug up and left in a pile if you want; water in child-sized watering cans; plastic containers for mixing soil and water; paint brushes; sticks and sponge squares; stiff card (one piece per child); antibacterial hand gel; wet wipes; bucket of water for rinsing hands; Bluetack.

Preparation:
Prepare the card for the children to use (cut-up cereal boxes or similar are good for this).

Make your mud, if you want to have it ready.

Procedure:
If the children will be mixing soil and water themselves to make mud, show them how to do this with a paintbrush, container, handful of soil and splash of water from one of the watering cans.

Talk out loud while you do it, e.g. "I'm just going to add a tiny bit of water and stir . . . I want my mud to be quite thick so that I can paint with it".

Demonstrate how to paint it onto the card, using a range of implements, such as a brush, a sponge, a stick or even your fingers.

When the paintings are done, the children can stick them up around the site with Bluetack before taking them home afterwards.

Practitioner's note:
You can provide "ready-mixed" mud if you like by making it in advance. Alternatively, give the children more scope for mess (and fun!) by providing plastic spades for them to dig up the soil and then mix it with water.

Make a Shaker

Activity type: Craft/creative

Age range: 2–3 years

Season: All year round

Resources: Empty yoghurt pots; circles of card; cut by tracing around the mouth of the pot; sellotape; things for putting inside; glue sticks for adding decorations to the outside (optional); scissors.

Preparation:
Cut the card circles, one per pot.
 Set up other resources.

Procedure:
Demonstrate how to make a shaker by choosing some interesting things and dropping them into a yoghurt pot. You only need a small handful – there needs to be plenty of space inside for shaking!
 Place a cardboard circle on top of the pot, and seal with sellotape so that it is securely fastened.
 If you want to decorate the pots, you could stick interesting leaves and flowers to the cardboard lid, or use crayons.
 Shake your shaker rhythmically, and comment on the type of sound that it makes, e.g. scratchy, heavy, high, low.

Practitioner's note:
Infants and young children put anything interesting in their mouths, so you must supervise your group very closely to ensure that they don't swallow anything that will be poisonous if uncooked. Avoid using dried beans, dried pasta or lentils, and instead use pebbles, gravel, dried leaves or broken twigs. The children will need help with using sellotape.

Forest Drums

Activity type: Craft/creative

Age range: 1–3 years

Season: All year round

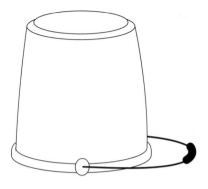

Resources: Sturdy sticks; thick slices of tree trunk/ log, or tree stumps still in the ground; logs, if you have any, of different lengths; different sized buckets, set upside down (optional); drum sticks or musical beaters, if you have access to these (bear in mind they might get scratched or dirty).

Preparation:
Set up the logs and trunk slices in a semi-circle shape, with a gap of half a metre or more between each one. Put the buckets out upside-down, if using.

Lay out a selection of beaters and sticks on the ground in front of them.

Procedure:
This is best as a free activity, where the children can choose a beater and then try out all the different forest drums.

Encourage them to talk about the sounds that they make, and the differences between the different beaters/sticks/drums.

You can lead a song, with the children beating the drums in accompaniment.

Practitioner's note:
Don't expect the children to have a well-developed sense of rhythm – just let them enjoy the sensation of hitting something repeatedly and joining in with the song at their own level.

Wallpaper Collage

Activity type: Craft/creative

Age range: 1–3 years

Season: All year round

Resources: Old roll of wallpaper; leaves, flowers, soil, weeds, or during the Winter try scraps of fabric, foil, feathers, paper, etc.; glue sticks.

Preparation:
Roll the wallpaper out wrong side up, so that the blank underside is the one you can see. Make sure that there is enough space for all the children to kneel down alongside it (more if they are all going to be accompanied by a parent).

Weigh down the corners with stones so that it doesn't roll up again, or tape them down if resting on tarmac.

Put any materials you are providing for the collage within easy reach of the wallpaper.

Draw any outline which you want the children to follow on the paper in black felt tip, such as a countryside scene of trees and flowers or an underwater scene of fishes and seaweed.

Procedure:
Explain to the children that they will be making a giant picture today. If you have provided a black outline on the paper, explain what it is to the children.

Collect some items to add to the collage, and stick them on, commenting out loud as you do about the choices you made, e.g. "I think that this will look really good up here because it's a bright green colour, like grass."

Encourage them to collect items and stick them on.

Practitioner's note:
This activity benefits from adults helping the children on a one-to-one basis, as they can help them to stick to the lines and make the finished collage look a bit better! But don't worry about the quality – the fun that the children are having is far more important.

Wall Weaving

Activity type: Craft/creative

Age range: 2–3 years

Season: All year round

Resources:
A chain-link fence/unused trellis/picket fence panel or living willow sculpture; plenty of long, narrow scraps of fabric, ribbon, crepe paper, wool, etc.

Preparation:
Cut your scraps (make sure each is about a metre long).

Decide which feature of the site you are going to use as the weaving frame, and make sure that it will be safe for the children to be working with.

Procedure:
Show the children how to "weave" a scrap of fabric through the fence by pushing the end through the holes away from you, then pulling it back through the next one. Repeat until you have "woven" most of your scrap through the holes.

Encourage the children to experiment with a range of the different scraps, to see which colours and textures they prefer.

Practitioner's note:
The children can find other things around the site to add to the weaving if they like too, such as sticks or twigs with leaves on them.

Check any fence or willow structure that you plan to use for stability before doing this activity.

Giant Painting

Activity type: Craft/creative

Age range: 1–3 years

Season: All year round

Resources: Roll of wallpaper; ready-mixed paints in different colours; paint brushes in different sizes; paint rollers, if you have some; water containers for rinsing the brushes out, if you want the children to do this (provide one for every two children).

Preparation:
Roll the wallpaper out wrong side up, so that the blank underside is the one you can see. Make sure that there is enough space for all the children to kneel down alongside it (more if they are all going to be accompanied by a parent).

Weigh down the corners with stones so that it doesn't roll up again, or tape them down if resting on tarmac.

Put any materials you are providing for the painting within easy reach of the wallpaper.

Draw any outline which you want the children to follow on the paper in black felt tip, such as a rainbow, or shapes. Keep it simple, because the rollers will make very large marks!

Procedure:
Explain what type of picture you will all be creating together, and then demonstrate how to use the different painting implements to colour it in.

Encourage the children to explore all the different colours and implements for making this communal painting.

Pasta Necklaces

Activity type: Craft/creative

Age range: 2–3 years (see Practitioner's Note below)

Season: All year round

Resources: Dried penne pasta, or another large type with holes through it; wool or string, cut into lengths of about 40cms.

Preparation:
Cut the wool or string in advance.

Put the pasta into containers so it is easy for the children to find and use.

Procedure:
Show the children how to thread pasta onto the string.

Tie the string in a knot around the first piece of pasta to stop it from falling off the other end. (You will need to do this for each child as they start, so if parents are in attendance enlist their help.)

Thread more pieces of pasta on until you have enough to tie both the ends together and make a necklace.

Ensure that you tell any parents in your group, or other adults working with you, that the children **must not** eat dried pasta.

Practitioner's note:
You can extend this activity by getting the children to paint their necklaces once they are finished. You will need to provide ready-mixed paint, brushes or sponge squares, and wet wipes/water in a bucket for rinsing hands if you do this.

Sparkling Pinecones

Activity type: Craft/creative

Age range: 1–3 years

Season: Winter

Resources: Pine cones; glue; glitter, sequins and other small sparkly decorations in different colours; string and sellotape.

Preparation:
Put the sequins, glitter etc. in shallow dishes which the children can dip their pine cone into.

Lay out the glue so it is easy to use.

Cut lengths of string for parents to attach to their child's cone with sellotape (they can do this if they want to turn it into a Christmas tree decoration).

Procedure:
Show the children how to put glue on their pinecone. Then dip it into the glitter and shake the loose pieces back into the dish. An adult helps to fix string to the base of the cone with sellotape. Finally, hang them up in a tree to admire.

Practitioner's note:
This activity is over very quickly – make sure you have plenty of pinecones to decorate, or have some suggestions of other things to do up your sleeve.

Finger Painting

Activity type: Craft/creative

Age range: 1–3 years

Season: All year round

Resources:
Ready-mixed paint; dishes for pouring the paint into (one dish per colour); wet wipes; bucket of water for rinsing hands; card or paper.

Preparation:
Set out the paint so that each colour is in a shallow dish or saucer.
Put the resources for cleaning fingers nearby.

Procedure:
Show the children how to dip your fingers into the paint and then make marks on the paper.

Show them also how to make shapes with their finger prints – demonstrate a few ideas such as a face, a tree and a rainbow.

Before the children start, tell the parents or other adults where the stuff for cleaning fingers is, and also ask the children to roll up their sleeves.

Practitioner's note:
The children will need one-to-one supervision during this activity to ensure that they don't get paint all over themselves.

Water Painting

Activity type: Craft/creative

Age range: 1–3 years

Season: Summer

Resources: Plenty of large paintbrushes, rollers and sponges; buckets or trays of water; food colouring (optional).

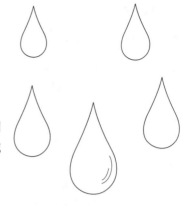

Preparation:
Fill a couple of large containers with water. They will
need to be wide enough for the children to dip their rollers or paintbrushes in.

If you want to add a few drops of food colouring to the water to tint it with a different colour, do so before the activity starts.
Set out any other resources required.

Procedure:
Explain to the children that you will be doing water painting, and show them what they can "paint". Choose a really large area, such as a fence, a brick wall or an area of tarmac.

Show the children how to dip the brushes and rollers into the water and then wipe across the area being painted. Tell them to try and paint as much of the space as they can, filling in any gaps.

Strictly speaking, you could do this activity all year round. The children are likely to get very wet, however, so it's best to reserve it for hot and sunny weather. If you do it in colder weather, the children **must** wear waterproofs to prevent their clothing from becoming wet (see Chapter 5).

Laying Trails

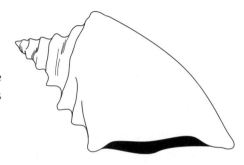

Activity type: Craft/creative

Age range: 1–3 years (older children will be able to create the trails with help, whereas younger ones can follow them).

Season: All year round

Resources:
Anything which is appropriate for children to use and can be laid in a trail. For example: rope; large shells (these must be too big for a child to put in their mouth); stones; plastic balls for a ball pit; twigs; beanbags; large coloured feathers.

Preparation:
The idea of this is to lay a trail which will lead the group to another activity, such as a book for a story, or a role play area set up in the trees.

With this in mind, create a winding path across the ground for the children to follow. Try to obscure the thing that they will find behind trees, bushes or some portable screening. This will maintain the surprise.

Procedure:
Show the children the trail and explain why they need to follow it.

If you choose to lead the group, you can control the speed at which they move along the trail by telling a story as they go, or incorporating a game of Follow the Leader with simple movements for them to copy.

Practitioner's note:
You can enhance this activity by including play tunnels or hanging hoops for the children to climb through as part of the trail, or ask them to collect a particular type of object whenever they see it.

Leaf Patterns

Activity type: Craft/creative

Age range: 1–3 years

Season: Late Spring to late Autumn

Resources: Plenty of leaves!

Preparation:
Note if there are any bushes or trees which the children
should not take leaves from.
If the leaves on your site are growing out of the children's reach, carefully cut a few branches down with loppers and then lay them on the ground so that the children can pick leaves off them.

Spend a few minutes making some patterns with leaves on the ground, such as a circle, triangle, a sunshine or zigzag.

Procedure:
Show the children the pattern that you have made on the ground using leaves. Feel free to incorporate your pattern into a story or theme that you might be using.
Invite the children to make their own patterns like yours by collecting leaves and arranging them on the ground.

It's fine for the children to come up with their own designs too – but by keeping it simple at the beginning they will understand what the activity is about before beginning to experiment.

Move around the site looking at what they are making, and invite the other children/parents to take a look at the patterns and pictures being created.

Practitioner's note:
For the best variety of colour, try this activity in early Autumn when the leaves are beginning to turn.

Autumn Rainbows

Activity type: Craft/creative

Age range: 1–3 years

Season: Autumn

Resources: One roll of old wallpaper or large pieces of card (one per child); glue sticks; plenty of Autumn leaves; picture of a rainbow (in a storybook or printed from the internet).

Preparation:
If using wallpaper to make a large, communal rainbow, unroll it so that the plain side is facing upwards. Weigh down the corners with stones, or tape them down to the ground so that it doesn't roll up again.

Sketch a rainbow outline on the wallpaper. Write which colour goes in which stripe if you wish.

If using individual pieces of card, ensure that you have one per person prepared.

Procedure:
Talk to the children about rainbows and ask them what colours you can see in them. If you want, show them a picture of one to ensure that they know what you're referring to.

Tell them that we will be making a rainbow of our own, using leaves of all different colours.

Model how to find a particular colour – e.g. yellow – and then stick on the rainbow outline. Discuss other colours you can find with the children and accompanying adults – green, red, orange, brown.

Children can collect leaves of all colours, and then add them to the collage. It might be worth asking the adults to ensure that the children stick the leaves down in stripes of colour, e.g. all yellows in one stripe, all greens in another, etc.

Practitioner's note:
If it is quite a damp day, advise the children and accompanying adults to find dry leaves – ones that are hanging on trees – as the wet surfaces will be hard to stick to the paper.

Leaf Flowers

Activity type: Craft/creative

Age range: 1–3 years

Season: Late Spring to late Autumn

Resources: Plenty of leaves, in different shapes and colours; pieces of card (roughly A4 size); glue sticks; Bluetack.

Preparation:
Put the card and glue sticks out, ready to use.

Procedure:
Show the children how to stick different coloured leaves to a piece of card to make a flower shape.

Children collect their own leaves and make their own designs – the youngest will definitely need one-to-one support with this activity.

When finished, invite the children to stick their work up to the walls or on the trunks of trees using Bluetack.

Practitioner's note:
This activity does not take very long, so make sure you have extra pieces of card for early finishers to make another design.

If you have no card, you could also do this activity on the ground, with the children making flower shapes on grass or tarmac. Choose a day with no wind for this.

Going Camping!

Activity type: Craft/creative

Age range: 2–3 years

Season: All year round

Resources: Some tents to play in – sun tents, play tents, tunnel tents or home-made ones using a blanket or sheet hung over a rope; a few props, such as cushions, scraps or fabric, pots and pans, a cuddly toy.

Preparation:
Set up the tent(s) in an area of your site.
  Hide the props a little further away for the children to find later.

Procedure:
Tell the children that you are all going camping today and either lead them to the tent if you have a small site, or ask them to find it if you have a larger one.
  Once they have explored inside the tent(s), ask them what they would bring camping to make it more comfy in there. Listen to their suggestions and then ask them to have a good look around and bring anything they find which they think will be useful.
  Let the children arrange things inside the tent and generally play for as long as they are interested in it!

Practitioner's note:
When hiding objects for them to use, feel free to include items that they can find a use for, such as a cardboard box or square of fabric, as well as more recognisable things such as a cushion.

Making Forest Soup

Activity type: Craft/creative

Age range: 1–3 years

Season: All year round, but best from mid Spring to late Autumn

Resources: Buckets or containers (enough for one per child); wooden or plastic spoons (one per child); water in child-sized watering cans; plenty of natural materials, such as leaves, flowers, sticks, stones etc.; "recipe cards" with ingredients for the soup written on them (optional – see Practitioner's Note below).

Preparation:
If using recipe cards, place them around the site for the children to find.
    Set out all other resources required for this activity.

Procedure:
In essence, you're going to show the children and accompanying adults how to make a "soup" from interesting things that they can find on the site and water from the watering cans.
    Model how to find interesting things, such as odd-shaped leaves or daisy heads, and show how to add them to your bucket, add water from the watering cans and stir with the spoon.
    Bear in mind that the watering cans will run out quite quickly – have someone tasked with refilling them, or do it yourself (while leaving another member of staff in charge).

Practitioner's note:
You can extend this activity by making recipe cards which list the things that the children need to find to make the soup. You can make this list with pictures for the children to identify or words for an adult to read to them.
    Stress that the children mustn't try and eat their soup, because Forest Soup is made for animals from things that we don't eat.

Making a Cooking Fire

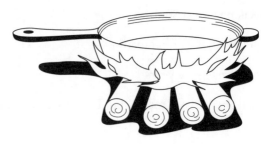

Activity type: Craft/creative

Age range: 1–3 years

Season: All year round, but nice to do
this in the Winter

Resources: Plenty of sticks; some saucepans or pots

Preparation: None

Procedure:
Explain to the children that we are going to make our own pretend fires today. If it's
Winter, talk about how fires can keep us warm and how searching for the sticks can
warm our bodies up.

   Show the children how to find sticks to make a pretend fire. Talk out loud about what
you're doing – "this is a good long stick, I'll use this one here . . . . This is a short one, I'll
lay that one across the top like this . . .".

   Encourage them to explore the site and find sticks from all around – this is a nice way
for them to look around the corners they don't usually play in.

   If it's Autumn, find orange leaves to sprinkle on top of the fire for the flames.

Practitioner's note:
This activity works nicely with Making Forest Soup – the children can make their fires
and pretend to cook their soup on them.

Windy Day Rockets

Activity type: Craft/creative

Age range: 1–3 years

Season: All year round

Resources: Toilet roll tubes or kitchen roll tubes (one per child); lots of strips of crêpe paper, tissue paper in different colours (15–20cms long, 2cm wide); glue sticks; sellotape; readymade nose cones (cut round a circle 10cms in diameter, then make a cut from the edge into the middle. Curve one edge under the other to make a cone shape, and tape together); string to hang them from trees (one length about 30cm per rocket); scissors (for cutting the rockets down at the end of the session).

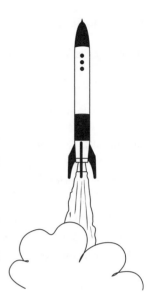

Preparation:
Make the nose cones and cut the string and strips of paper in advance.

Make a rocket yourself before the session starts so you can show it to the children and other adults.

Procedure:
Show the children how to stick strips of crêpe paper or tissue paper to one end of the tube, trying to leave no gaps.

Next, show how to choose and stick a nose cone on to the other end.

Finally, attach one end of a piece of string to the body of the rocket (sellotape is handy here) and then the children can find somewhere to tie their rocket so it will fly in the breeze.

Practitioner's note:
Children will enjoy this but will need assistance with some of the fiddly aspects, such as tying the string to a branch or sticking the strips accurately to the end of the tube.

If you want to extend this activity, the children could also decorate the body of their rocket by sticking things to the sides of the tube.

Woodland Skittles

Activity type: Craft/creative

Age range: 2–3 years

Season: All year round

Resources: Transparent plastic drink bottles, labels removed (one per child); water tinted with food colouring; plenty of things that are small enough to poke into the mouth of a bottle: gravel, acorns, twigs, leaves, etc.; a "bowling ball" (beachball or larger); funnel for pouring the water; glitter (optional).

Preparation:
Tint the water you will be using.

Lay out any resources that you want to provide.

Procedure:
Explain that we will be making skittles today. Show how to choose things small enough to poke into the bottle – you will probably want to give the children time here to explore the site and find things to use.

Once the children have some things in their bottles, show them how to add a sprinkle of glitter to the contents, and then add water by using the funnel.

Help the children to secure the lids very tightly, and then line up the skittles for a game.

Take turns to roll the ball at the skittles, seeing if you can touch one of them or knock them over.

Practitioner's note:
Children will need supervision with this activity to ensure that they are not picking sharp or stinging materials such as nettles, or trying to drink the contents. Fasten them securely and add sellotape around the lid if you wish.

The skittles will need to be set up quite close to the children, no more than three or four metres away, so they have a chance of rolling the ball towards them.

Mega Painting

Activity type: Craft/creative

Age range: 1–3 years

Season: All year round

Resources: Wallpaper; paint brushes of all sizes, sponge pieces, rollers; ready-mixed paint in different colours; water pots for rinsing paintbrushes (optional); wet wipes; bucket of water for rinsing hands.

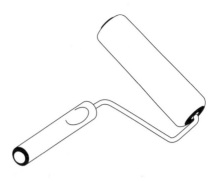

Preparation:
Unroll the wallpaper along the ground so that the reverse is facing upwards, making sure that there is enough space for everyone to kneel along the edge. Weigh down the corners with stones.

Put the paint into wide, shallow dishes which the children can dip their brushes into. Lay out any brushes and implements they can use.

If you want the children to make one communal picture, sketch an outline of it onto the wallpaper in black felt tip. Otherwise leave it blank.

Procedure:
Tell the children that we're going to do a mega painting today, where everyone works on the same giant piece of paper. If you have a theme for the mega painting, explain it briefly here (e.g. link it to the story you have just read).

If you want the all children to attempt the same design, e.g. a butterfly, then model how to paint one before they start.

Let the children experiment with different colours and brush types.

Practitioner's note:
If you want to avoid the children rinsing their brushes during the activity, then allocate a couple of brushes per colour, and have them take turns in using the different colours.

Footprint/Handprint Heaven

Activity type: Craft/creative

Age range: 1–3 years

Season: Summer

Resources: Ready-mixed paint in shallow dishes, three different colours; paint brushes; wallpaper; wet wipes; old towels; paddling pool/water tray for rinsing hands and feet in.

Preparation:
Fill the paddling pool (or equivalent) half full.

Pour paint into shallow dishes and put one or two paint brushes with each colour. Spread out the wallpaper per instructions for Mega Painting.

Procedure:
Explain to the children and adults that we are making a print picture today using our hands/feet/both!

Model how to make a hand print by choosing a paint colour, painting your hand with a paintbrush and then choosing somewhere to print it on the paper.

Show how to rinse the paint off in the rinsing pool and dry your hands on the old towels you have provided. Explain how to do a foot print if appropriate.

As the adults/parents help their children, ensure there is enough paint, and keep an eye on whether the water in the rinsing pool needs changing.

Practitioner's note:
This activity benefits from one-to-one supervision, especially when the children are putting their socks and shoes back on.

Children must never be allowed to play in or by a paddling pool unsupervised – ensure that there is always an adult present.

Tunnels, Tents and Torches

Activity type: Craft/creative

Age range: 1–3 years

Season: All year round

Resources: Two or three torches; any or all of the following: a tent, a play tun-nel, makeshift shelter made from blankets and ropes.

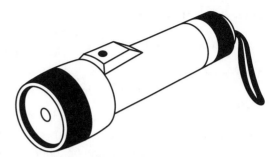

Preparation:
Set up an interesting area for the children to explore with the torches. You will want to create places which are shaded or hidden, such as spaces inside tents, bushes or tunnels.

If you have a path through some shrubbery, you can mark this for the children to explore by laying a rope down for them to follow.

Procedure:
Explain to the children that they will be exploring a special area with torches, so that they can see in the dark.

Lead them around, giving them plenty of time to explore.

Practitioner's note:
If you are running this activity repeatedly, consider hiding something special in the tent or tunnel which the children have to look for – you can put it back again before the next group start.

If you are running a parent and toddler group, consider asking the parents to bring a torch to the next session when you run this activity, so that all the children have their own torch.

Crepe Paper Streamers

Activity type: Craft/creative

Age range: 1–3 years

Season: All year round

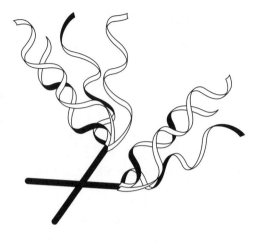

Resources: Whole roll of crepe paper, cut into strips 4cm wide; sticks – one per child, 20–30cm long and quite straight.

Preparation:
Cut the crêpe paper into strips 4cm wide and the length of the roll of crêpe paper.

Procedure:
Show the children how to make a streamer.

Unravel the end of the crêpe paper strip and carefully stick it to the end of a stick with sellotape.

Unravel the rest of the paper strip and whirl around your head to make shapes in the air. To make a multi-coloured one, sellotape two streamers on your stick, both of different coloured crêpe paper.

Show the children how to run around the site with their streamers, whirling them in circles in front of their bodies or making shapes with them in the air.

Practitioner's note:
Make sure that the children stand some distance apart when playing with their streamers so that they don't poke each other in the face with their sticks.

Sticky Forest Flags

Activity type: Craft/creative

Age range: 1–3 years

Season: Spring to late Autumn (see Practitioner's Note below)

Resources: Sticks – one per child; rectangles of fabric or paper – one per child; glue sticks; plenty of natural resources, such as leaves, grasses and flowers; sellotape and scissors.

Preparation:
Put the glue sticks out and ensure you have enough paper or fabric.

Procedure:
Show the children how to make a sticky forest flag.

First they need to find a stick that's roughly as long as their arm.

Then they need to decorate the fabric/paper with pretty leaves etc. from the site – show how to use glue to stick these on to the surface.

Finally, use the sellotape to fasten the flag to the stick. The children can find somewhere interesting on the site to display their flag afterwards.

Practitioner's note:
A Winter version of this activity could be providing a rectangle of plain fabric for the children to paint before fastening it to a stick to make a flag, as above.

If using paint, remember to provide wet wipes and a bucket of water for rinsing fingers afterwards.

Magical Shields

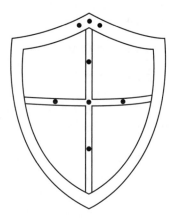

Activity type: Craft/creative

Age range: 1–3 years

Season: All year round

Resources: Paper plates (one per child); ready-mixed paint and brushes or glue sticks for sticking on leaves; strips of card to stick on the back for a handle; sellotape and scissors.

Preparation:
Cut the strips of card for the handles.
    Set out the resources.

Procedure:
Show the children how to make a magic shield.
    First, gather some interesting leaves to stick to the front of the paper plate.
    Next, take a strip of card and carefully stick each end to the back of the plate, leaving a gap so that you can hold onto it. Sellotape will work better than glue here.
    After the children have finished, let them test whether their magical shield will help them hide in the woods. Find a good hiding place and hold the shield up in front of you . . . . Can the grown-ups find you?

Practitioner's note:
If you are doing this in Winter you can use paint instead. Be sure to let the paint dry before letting the children play with their shields.

Animal Shelters

Activity type: Craft/creative

Age range: 2–3 years

Season: Late Spring to late Autumn

Resources: Plenty of natural materials such as twigs, leaves, grass, weeds, flowers, soil, stones, etc.

Preparation:
Make a little shelter that you can show the children, so that they know what you are talking about. If you have a toy animal to hide in it, add that too so they can see how an animal could live in a shelter.

Procedure:
Show the children the shelter that you have made earlier – something quite simple like sticks leaning against a fence with a covering of torn grass or leaves. Ask them to guess who lives there and what they like about it.

Tell the children that they will be making more little houses like this for animals to sleep in, and show them the kinds of things they could use (this is also for the benefit of the adults, so they know what kinds of things to use). Point out any nettles or brambles which people should avoid touching.

Encourage the children to collect things and build a little house. They will probably do something quite figurative, and that's fine – they will really enjoy the process of looking for things and finding a use for them.

When the children have all finished, you can do a little "walking tour" around the site with the group to take a look at everyone's shelter.

Practitioner's note:
The idea here is to encourage the children to make a little shelter from whatever they can find for an animal to use. This activity does not teach them facts about where certain animals live, but rather it lets them use their imaginations and feel purposeful.

Making a Nest

Activity type: Craft/creative

Age range: 1–3 years

Season: All year round

Resources: Plenty of natural materials: sticks, twigs, grass cuttings, leaves, etc.

Preparation:
Build a couple of "nests" on the ground where the children can see them, out of a range of things – twigs, grass and so on – to give them ideas about what to use. If flowers are available, use some to decorate them.

Procedure:
Lead the children over to the nests and ask them to guess what they are (give them a clue by saying that birds like to sit in them).

Explain that the children are going to try and make some nests for a big family of birds who need some extra space for all their baby birds. Talk about what things you have used in your nests and indicate where the children can collect things from on the site.

Let the children build their own nests (they will need some adult help) and if you have some toy birds, let them place one in their nest afterwards to test it out.

Making Dens

Activity type: Craft/creative

Age range: 2–3 years (see Practitioner's Note)

Season: All year round

Resources: Plastic crates, ropes (tied above head height by an adult), blankets, sheets, logs, large cardboard boxes, play tunnels, etc.

Preparation:
If you want you can set up a small den using some of the equipment to give the children an idea of what you mean.

Procedure:
The idea of this activity is to help the children set up a den with interesting places to sit, crawl and hide. They can then play in and around their den.

   The play is as important as creating the den here, so don't worry if you feel that it was mostly done by the adults – as the children become familiar with the activity, they will respond more to questions such as, "where do you think we should put this blanket?" before finally giving specific instructions about what they want!

Practitioner's note:
Young children who are very mobile will enjoy this activity, but children who cannot walk independently may find it a bit challenging. See Playing Tents for an idea which suits them better.

Playing Tents

Activity type: Craft/creative

Age range: 1–2 years

Season: All year round

Resources: As above

Preparation:
Set up a simple den for the children to play in. As long as it is safe, you can make it as ambitious as you like!

Procedure:
Show the children the den and invite them to crawl around inside it. Make sure that it is tall enough in some places for an adult to crawl in and sit alongside the children. Invite the children to find things to make it comfy, or to decorate it, and bring them inside.

Making a Butterfly

Activity type: Craft/creative

Age range: 1–3 years

Season: Best in late Spring to late Autumn

Resources: Outline of a butterfly's wings, drawn on A4 size card and cut out (one per child); string, about 70cms long, tied and then stuck to the back of the butterfly card in a figure of 8 shape with a piece of tape in the middle; glue sticks; plenty of leaves, flowers, grasses etc.

Preparation:
Prepare the butterfly wings as above (one per child)
    Hide the butterfly wings around the site.

Procedure:
Tell the children they will be making butterfly wings today, but first they have to find them because they have all blown away!
    When the children all have a set, show them how to stick interesting flowers, leaves etc. to the wings to decorate them.
    When the children have finished, they can slip their arms through the two loops of string on the back and wear their wings. Can they fly like a butterfly? What about a running race?

Practitioner's note:
This activity is brilliant on a breezy day, as the wings will flap as the children run.

Forest Telescopes

Activity type: Craft/creative

Age range: 1–3 years

Season: Late Spring to Autumn

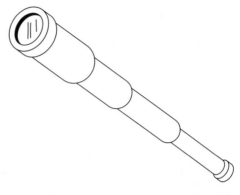

Resources: Toilet roll tubes or kitchen roll tubes (one per child); glue sticks; plenty of natural materials such as leaves, flowers and grasses; small elastic bands (one per telescope); squares of coloured cellophane – plastic wrappers from sweets or chocolates are perfect for this (one per telescope).

Preparation:
Set out any resources needed.

Procedure:
Show the children how to make a forest telescope by covering the sides of their tube in interesting things that they find.

Show how to fit a coloured lens by fitting one of the cellophane squares over the end with an elastic band.

The children can then use their telescopes to investigate the site. What can they see? What do they notice?

Practitioner's note:
You don't need to add the lenses to the telescope if you don't have any cellophane.

Camouflage Hats

Activity type: Craft/creative

Age range: 1–3 years

Season: Late Spring to late Autumn

Resources: Newspaper, folded into a
simple "hat" shape (the same shape as when you make a newspaper boat); glue sticks;
plenty of leaves, flowers, etc.; sellotape (optional).

Preparation:
Fold the newspaper sheets in advance, one per child.
    Set out any other resources required.

Procedure:
Explain that you are going to make a hat which helps you hide in the woods today.
    Show the children how to stick interesting things on to their newspaper hats. Encourage them to explore the site looking for interesting things to use.
    Once all the children have finished, let them test whether their hats let them hide by asking the grown-ups to count to ten while their children run off to hide in the trees!
    (Some children won't want to do this without their parents – that's fine, you can change the game so the parent and child hide together if that works better.)

Practitioner's note:
Use sellotape to secure the hats – they sometimes have a habit of unfolding while a child is wearing them!

Forest Birthday Cakes

Activity type: Craft/creative

Age range: 1–3 years

Season: All year round

Resources: Buckets (one per child); toy animal; something for stirring, e.g. wooden spoon, stick (one per child); child-sized watering cans; plenty of natural materials: soil, gravel, grass, weeds, etc.; birthday cake candles (one per child); small plastic bowls or silicone cake cases (one per child).

Preparation:
Set out the equipment you will use.

Procedure:
Explain that the children will be making a birthday cake for an animal in the woods today (choose which one). Stress that this is not the kind of cake that we can eat because it is a forest cake for animals.

Show how to collect interesting things in the bucket and then turn into a cake mixture by adding water and stirring with a stick or a spoon.

Pour some of the mixture into a small plastic bowl/silicone cake case and then place a candle in the top.

Sing happy birthday!

Songs

Singing with children is always great fun, and there are plenty of songs you could use in your sessions. Bear in mind that parents can sometimes be a bit shy about joining in, so you – and any other adults working with you – are likely to be the only voices singing for the first few lines!

These songs are all great fun:

- Heads, shoulders, knees and toes
- In and out the dusty bluebells
- Old MacDonald had a farm
- Ring o' roses
- Hey diddle diddle
- Baa baa black sheep
- Five little speckled frogs
- Zoom zoom zoom, we're going to the moon
- There were five in the bed
- Wind the bobbin up

Try looking online if you're not sure of the exact lyrics or tune of any of the above. Also, use any others that you know are familiar to your group.

Planning activities for one year olds (infants)

There's a big difference between what a one year old and a three year old can do, and yet we're putting them together in our outdoor toddler group! Do we need two sets of plans?

If you are running a group where parents stay for the session, you can assume that parents will support their children with all the activities. This means that, as long as you choose your activities carefully, you don't need a separate programme for the infants.

If, on the other hand, you don't have one-to-one support for your youngest children, you may want to plan separate activities for them. This will ensure that they are able to access things at their level and get the most from their session. Choose an area of the site which is relatively secluded and set it up for them to explore and play in, with supervision from another adult, per required adult-to-child ratio. The following are a few ideas for what to put in this area.

Baby Obstacle Course

Activity type: Infants

Age range: 12–18 months

Season: All year round

Resources:
Play tunnel, hoops laid on the floor, cushions to crawl over, blanket spread across the ground, logs/tree stumps to touch and pull themselves up on, etc.

Preparation:
Set up an area filled with interesting things for the babies in your group to crawl around and investigate. Include things with different textures, like wood, plastic, fabric.

Procedure:
Let the babies crawl around and explore their area with supervision from adults. Encourage them to touch, move and lift things – it's fine if the area is somewhat rearranged by them!

Practitioner's note:
Don't forget that the natural environment of grass, shrubs and trees also provides interesting textures to explore. Also, gently sloping or uneven ground is quite exciting for them to investigate.

Baby Camping

Activity type: Infants

Age range: 12–18 months

Season: All year round

Resources: Sun tents or tents made from sheets hung over a rope tied to two uprights; a few props inside the tents, such as cushions, pots and pans, toys.

Preparation:
Set up your tents and put a few interesting things inside them for the children to discover.

Procedure:
Let the babies explore the tents, crawling in and out of them, with adult supervision.

Practitioner's note:
This activity provides shelter on a hot sunny day for your littlest children.

Treasure Baskets

Activity type: Infants

Age range: 12–18 months

Season: All year round

Resources: Ten or so resources, chosen according to a theme, in a basket or open box.

Preparation:
Choose a theme for your treasure basket and collect the items together. There are plenty of ideas online, but some ideas are given below to get you started:

- Kitchen: wooden spoon, whisk, empty ice cube tray, set of measuring spoons, various plastic bowls, doilies, fly covers, colander.
- Textures: large squares of fake fur, velour, laminated material, knitting, cotton handkerchief, leather or leatherette, sponge, etc.
- Things that make a sound: toy tambourine, different shakers, maracas, measuring spoons, whistle, toy drum, etc.

Procedure:
Put the treasure basket in a quiet area of the site if you are using activity zoning, so that the infants can explore the contents and crawl around without being in the way of the older children. Ensure that they are supervised by an adult if parents are not in attendance.

Practitioner's note:
The point of treasure baskets is to give infants a range of interesting items to explore through manipulation and handling.

Infants often put interesting things in their mouths – for this reason, choose only things which are suitable. No sharp points or edges, or fragile materials such as glass.

Don't worry about including items which are not "natural"; this is an activity to complement the exploration and play that they have outside, not to replace it.

Forest Bath-Time

Activity type: Infants

Age range: 12–18 months

Season: All year round

Resources: A paddling pool, half full; a range of objects
and toys to float on the water – pine cones, bath toys,
wooden blocks, empty plastic bottles with or without
lids on, sticks *or* a range of different shaped containers
such as squeezy bottles, washed yoghurt pots, funnels, sieves, bottles, buckets, trays
etc.

Preparation:
Position the paddling pool in a corner of your site and fill.
    Set out the objects for floating.

Procedure:
Show the children how to put things into the pool and let them explore and play with
them, investigating whether they float or sink or take on water.
    Alternatively they can experiment with filling and emptying containers.

Practitioner's note:
If it's a hot day, you can provide old towels for drying and advise parents to bring a
change of clothes so that their children can enter the paddling pool.
    Always supervise paddling pools closely and never leave a child playing unattended
by or in one.

Using storybooks

Planning activities linked to the theme or characters of a storybook is a great way to run your sessions. Finding the book can be part of the fun for the children, if you hide it and give them clues about where to look for it. Sit everyone in a circle to listen to the story, and make sure that you read it clearly with the pages facing the children so that they can see the pictures. Below are a few well-known children's books which have an outdoor theme.

- *Norman, the Slug With the Silly Shell* by Sue Hendra
- *The Very Hungry Caterpillar* by Eric Carle
- *Beautiful Bananas* by Elizabeth Laird
- *Over in the Clover* by Jan Omerod
- *Stickman* by Julia Donaldson
- *The Gruffalo* by Julia Donaldson
- *We're Going on a Bearhunt* by Michael Rosen
- *Owl Babies* by Martin Waddell
- *Farmer Duck* by Martin Waddell

Of course, there's always traditional tales such as The Three Little Pigs, Little Red Riding Hood and The Billy Goats Gruff, which you can tell with hand puppets.

Thematic planning

Thematic planning is choosing your activities around a theme. The theme can come from anywhere and storybooks are really useful because you can use aspects of the story, or one of the main characters, to devise all your activities. I have given two examples of thematic planning for a session below.

Owl Babies by Martin Waddell is the story of three baby owls who live in a tree and wake up one night to find that their mother is missing.

As they wait for her to return, they speculate about what has happened to her. Once the story has been read to the children, they could build nests for other baby owls to stay in if they have lost their mummy. They could also make a giant collage of an owl using different coloured leaves for the feathers. If you have a cuddly toy or hand puppet in the shape of an owl you could hide it and the children – as the owl babies – could try to find it.

Stickman by Julia Donaldson is the story of a stick man who is unwittingly whisked away from his family home on a series of adventures. As he is taken further and further away from his family, he becomes more desperate, until he makes it back home on Christmas Eve. The children could look at the pictures in the book of Stickman's home, and build their own version out of twigs, leaves and other natural materials. They could then make their own Stickman from sticks tied together with string before taking him on some new adventures around the site, such as playing in the paddling pool or playing hide and seek.

9 | Useful links

In this chapter we will look at links for:

- sources of funding;
- equipment providers;
- finding a site;
- guidance on tax, self-employment and employing others;
- obtaining a Disclosure and Barring Service check (formerly known as CRB check);
- first aid training and safeguarding;
- guidance on the Early Years Foundation Stage framework;
- insurers specialising in childcare settings;
- developing your activity area;
- further activity ideas;
- Forest School training.

The links in this chapter are intended as a starting point rather than an exhaustive list, and were all correct when this book was printed. Since then, some of the initiatives offered may have changed.

Sources of funding

Awards for All

Awards for All provides Lottery-funded grants from £300 to £10,000 for community groups and projects, subject to the application meeting the regional outcome requirements displayed on the website.
http://www.awardsforall.org.uk

People's Health Trust

This is the funding arm of the Health Lottery. An initiative called Active Communities offers grants of between £5,000 to £25,000 for larger, ongoing projects which aim to reduce health inequality for the people living in more deprived areas of the UK and improve community links.
http://www.peopleshealthtrust.org.uk/

Equipment providers

There will be many and varied suppliers online; these are just a few to get you started.
Muddy Faces have a huge range of outdoor goods for children to use, excellent prices for small budgets and prompt despatch.
http://www.muddyfaces.co.uk

Early Excellence offers a special range of treasure baskets and equipment sets for children aged 6 months to 3 years.
http://www.earlyexcellence.com

Hopscotch School Supply provides a range of resources to nurseries and schools.
http://www.hopscotchschoolsupply.com

Wriggly Wrigglers provides seeds, birdfeed, bird boxes, composting equipment and advice for developing your site.
http://www.wigglywigglers.co.uk

Finding a site

Scout huts, church halls, WI halls, community centres . . .

Track down a contact name and number by looking up your local facilities online. Alternatively, find a local community forum and see what other places are listed.

Local parks authority

You can contact your local parks manager through your local council, and they will be able to advise you on parks and recreational areas which you could use. They should also be able to advise you of any permits you might need to purchase and restrictions on activities.

Farms and city farms

Some farms welcome the use of their land by children's groups as it allows them to introduce children to the world of farming and obtain some funding in return.

Try doing a websearch for city farms or community farms in your area, as these will already be switched on to the idea of children's activities onsite.

These links may also be useful:

* http://www.farmgarden.org.uk
* http://www.farmsforschools.org.uk
* http://www.countrysidelearning.org

Nature reserves

Natural England offers a wealth of guidance including lists of local nature reserves.
http://www.naturalengland.org.uk

Play England has an interactive map to find the nearest natural play space.
http://www.playengland.org.uk

Green Flag Award sites are local nature reserves or conservation areas which have ongoing programmes of community activities and welcome local participation.
http://greenflag.keepbritaintidy.org/award-winning-sites/

Wildlife Trust

There are forty-seven different wildlife trusts across Britain and many have innovative activities for children and families already running.
http://www.wildlifetrusts.org

National Trust

The National Trust are a major landowner in the UK and have a policy of encouraging local participation and usage through public engagement. Contact your regional headquarters to find out about natural play areas which may available for use, or opportunities to use the grounds of some stately homes.

Guidance on tax, self-employment and paying others

Her Majesty's Revenue and Customs (HMRC)

If you are setting up your own business, you will need to contact the tax office to register yourself and find out how to declare your earnings. You will also need their guidance on the rules and regulations for employing other people.

You will be able to find out about tax workshops being held in your local area too.
http://www.hmrc.gov.uk/

Advice for setting up a business

This government-produced website offers a wealth of information and links to help you over the hurdles of setting up and marketing your own business.
https://www.gov.uk/browse/business/setting-up

Disclosure and Barring Service (formerly CRB checks)

This is the government website for obtaining a DBS check for anyone who will work with the children in your toddler group. These checks used to be called Criminal Records Bureau checks, hence the old acronym "CRB".

The site gives advice on the documentation required, the process and the time it will take to complete.
https://www.gov.uk/disclosure-barring-service-check/overview

First aid training

St. John's Ambulance provides a two-day Early Years first aid course for people working with pre-school children which meets Ofsted requirements for childminders and nannies. The website has primers for cuts, fractures, shock and bleeding as well as a downloadable first aid app for mobile phones.
http://www.sja.org.uk/sja/first-aid-advice.aspx

Specialised first aid training is available for working with young children in remote outdoor areas; try doing a websearch for paediatric first aid outdoors. Two providers are given below, but there are plenty more online.
http://www.itcfirstaid.org.uk
http://www.acornsafety.co.uk

Safeguarding children

This website offers advice, based on current legislation, on a wide range of child safeguarding matters. The ratio of adults to children for various activities, different levels of DBS checks required, and codes of practice are all explained.
http://www.safenetwork.org.uk

Early Years Foundation Stage statutory framework

The department for Education website has links to this site, which acts as a place for sharing best practice as well as where to find the official documents laying out the framework.

You can find out more here about the early learning goals and how your activities will feed into them as the children attending your group progress.
http://www.foundationyears.org.uk/

Alternatively you can refer to the Department of Education website for the latest updates on policy changes:
http://www.gov.uk/government/organisations/department-for-education

Insurers specialising in childcare settings

Morton Michel

A professionally run and helpful company which offers a huge range of insurance to childcarers and childcare settings. It also gives customers access to free online childcare magazines full of activity ideas and training information about the Early Years Foundation Stage framework.

Developing your grounds

Learning through Landscapes

The Learning through Landscapes charity provides a wealth of useful information and a consultancy service where outdoor learning and landscaping experts will advise you on how to develop your grounds.

Their website includes guides on how to adapt and enhance your school grounds without recourse to paying for consultancy, staff training, resource ideas and advice on corporate partnerships.
http://www.ltl.org.uk

Woodland Trust

The Woodland Trust has regular giveaways of tree-planting packs for schools and community groups. Bear in mind that whatever you plant will take a few years to establish itself.
http://www.woodlandtrust.org.uk/plant-trees/

Wildlife gardening

The Natural England website provides leaflets, top tips and a wildlife gardening forum to help you develop your grounds.
http://www.naturalengland.org.uk/advice/wildlifegardening/default.aspx

Willow structures

Living willow structures are amazing things for children to play in, and are relatively easy to plant and maintain. There are plenty of companies on the internet offering willow structure services. At the time of writing, the company below offers planting kits for domes, play tunnels and play dens.
http://www.thewillowbank.com

The Little Book of Outdoor Play by Sally Featherstone

This is a superb resource for people wanting to add plants and flowers to their site, with sections on different types of soil, aromatic plants, shade and sun-loving, and so on. It also includes ideas on creating borders and screens, plus plenty of activity ideas.

Further activity ideas

Juliet Robertson's Creative Star Learning blog

This is an invaluable resource for outdoor learning, featuring inspiring ideas as diverse as bird feeding, treasure hunts and junk orchestras.
http://creativestarlearning.co.uk/blog/

Nature Detectives

This website is an offshoot of the Woodland Trust and is a fantastic resource for activity ideas. The seasonal activity guides are also useful.
http://www.naturedetectives.org.uk/

Forest School training and forestry information

If you are interested in finding out more about the Forest Schools movement, including training opportunities near you, the Forestry Education Initiative website has a list of training providers. Each training organisation will have a slightly different take on the movement and its ethos, so it is advisable to check out the options available before choosing the course which fits your interests.

http://www.foresteducation.org/woodland_learning/forest_schools/training_providers/

Planning Template 1

Name of Group: .... Date/time of session: .... Risk assessment done: ....

Activity	Resources	Preparation
Health and safety notes		
Welcome activities e.g. singing welcome song, going over health and safety points for new parents		
Introduction e.g. a finding game, listening to a story, introducing the theme for today's session		
Activity 1		
Activity 2		
Free play/games		
Ending the session e.g. goodbye song		

Planning Template 2

Name of Group: .... Date/time of session: .... Risk assessment done: ....

Health and safety notes:

Shared activities to start: e.g. welcome song, listening to a story

ACTIVITY 1:	ACTIVITY 2:
Where?	Where?
Who?	Who?
Resources/preparation:	Resources/preparation:

ACTIVITY 3:	ACTIVITY 4:
Where?	Where?
Who?	Who?
Resources/preparation:	Resources/preparation:

Shared finish: e.g. goodbye song, games

Planning Template 3

Name of Group: .... Date/time of session: .... Risk assessment done: ....

Health and safety notes:

ACTIVITY 1:	ACTIVITY 2:
Where?	Where?
Who?	Who?
Resources/preparation:	Resources/preparation:
ACTIVITY 3:	ACTIVITY 4:
Where?	Where?
Who?	Who?
Resources/preparation:	Resources/preparation:

Assessment notes:

Appendix
Risk assessment grid

1. Use, add to or remove the risks listed below, as appropriate for your setting.
2. Then score the Probability of each risk from 1 to 5 (1 being very unlikely to 5 being unavoidable) and the Severity (1 not serious to 5 very serious).
3. Now multiply the Probability score for each risk with its Severity score, e.g. Probability of 2 x Severity of 3 = 6. Any risk with a PxS score of 12 or above must be dealt with immediately. Note any actions on your Risk Assessment grid, and tick them off once completed.

Group:................................. Leader:............................. Date:................

Location: ....

Section	Risk	Harm	Probability	Severity	P x S	Mitigation/by whom	Done
Site preparation	Touching broken glass or rusted metal	Cuts, infection				Litter pick by leader prior to session	
	Touching stinging nettles or bramble thorns	Rash or scratches				.	
Moving around site	Tripping over on uneven ground	Bruises, sprains				Leader to remind parents/children of risks at beginning of each session. Parents to supervise children.	
	Bumping into tree/each other	Bruises, concussion				Leader to remind parents/children to move safely around site at all times.	
	Dragging sticks and other materials	Facial injury, scratches				Leader to show children how to drag materials along the ground to avoid facial injuries. Leader to show where the stinging nettles and brambles are and advise not to touch.	
Canopy	Low-hanging dead branch, ready to fall out of tree	Head injury, concussion				Leader to inspect site and try to pull down any hanging dead wood prior to session.	
	Low branches	Concussion, bruising				Leader to note locations of low branches with children, and tie crepe strip around tip to ensure that they can be seen.	
	Twigs at eye-level	Facial injury, scratches				As above.	
Scrub	Stinging nettles/brambles	Rash or scratches				Clear the site of any growth that will hinder the children's access. Show children which plants to avoid touching.	
	Insects pollinating flowers	Bee sting/allergic reaction to insect bite				Leader to be aware of locations of flowering plants and remind the children to be careful. Leader to check medical notes for any children have allergic reaction to insect bites and stings.	

Category	Hazard	Risk	Control measure
Ground	Surface litter	Scratches, transfer of bacteria	Leader to remove any visible litter prior to session.
	Protruding roots/tree stump	Trips, slips and bruises	Leader and children to note location of roots/tree stumps and to move around the site carefully.
	Buried litter, including broken glass or rusty metal	Scratches, infection	Leader to inspect site for protruding, sharp litter and remove, where possible. Where not possible, leader to block off area so children do not come into contact with it.
Hygiene	Dirty hands from handling soil and natural materials	Stomach upsets, feeling ill	Leader to remind parents and children at the beginning of each session that food or drink should not be consumed during activities. Children reminded by leader to wash hands thoroughly at the end of session.
Injury and illness	Child X needs to use epipen	Fit, unconsciousness; Breathing difficulties	Leader to ask parents whether their child needs to use an epipen when they register for the group. Leader to request that parent brings an epipen to each session in the event that it is needed.
	Child X needs to use inhaler	Asthma attack, breathing difficulties	Leader to ask parents whether their child needs to use an inhaler when they register for the group. Leader to request that parent brings an inhaler to each session in the event that it is needed.

Bibliography

Bache, C. (2008) *Pre-school curriculum.* Fife: Secret Garden Outdoor Nursery.

Bilton, H. (2002) *Outdoor play in the early years: management and innovation.* London: David Fulton Publishing Ltd.

Bruner, J.S. (1983) *Child's talk: learning to use language.* New York: Norton.

Dahlgren, L. and Szczepanski, A. (1998) Outdoor education: an attempt at defining . . . *BSP Newsletter* 98 (20): 6–7.

Department for Education and Skills (2005) *Birth to three matters: an introduction to the framework.* Nottingham: DfES Publications.

Dewey, J. (1938) *Experience and education.* New York: Collier Books.

Featherstone, S. (2001) *The little book of outdoor play.* London: A and C Black Ltd.

Forestry Commission for Scotland (2005) Education strategy. *Woods for learning.* Edinburgh: Forestry Commission for Scotland.

Grahn, P., Martensoon, F., Lindblad, B., Nilsoon, P. and Ekman, A. (1997) *Ute pa dagis. Stad and Land, mr.145 [Outdoor daycare, city and country].* Hasselholm, Sweden: Norra Skane Offset.

Henninger, M. (1985) Preschool children's play behaviours in an indoor environment. In J. L. Frost and S. Sunderlin (Eds.) *When children play: proceedings of the International Conference on Play and Play Environments* (pp. 145–9). Wheaton, MD: Association for Child Education International.

Hopwood-Stephens, I. (2012) *Learning on your doorstep: stimulating writing through creative play outdoors for ages 5–9.* Oxford: Routledge.

Keenan, T. and Evans, S. (2009) *An introduction to child development.* London: Sage.

Lindon, J. (1999) Run the risk. *Nursery World,* Sep 23rd, 10–11.

Louv, R. (2008) *Last child in the woods: saving our children from nature deficit disorder.* New York: Algonquin Books.

Piaget, J. (1929) *The child's perception of the world.* New York: Harcourt, Brace and Co.

Pilsbury, R. (2008) *Forest school briefing paper.* Wolverhampton City Council.

Robertson, J. (2008) *I Ur Och Skur/Rain or shine: Swedish forest school.* London: Creative Learning Company.

Taylor, A. F., Wiley, A., Kuo, F.E. and Sullivan, W.C. (1998) Growing up in the inner city: green spaces as places to grow. *Environment and Behavior* (30): 3–27.

Vygotsky, L.S. (1978) *Mind and society: the development of higher psychological processes.* Cambridge, MA: Harvard University Press.

Wellman, H. M. (1990) *The child's theory of mind.* Cambridge, MA: MIT Press.